VISIBLE CHURCH—VISIBLE UNITY

Ecumenical Ecclesiology and
"The Great Tradition of the Church"

Ola Tjørhom

Foreword by
Geoffrey Wainwright

LITURGICAL PRESS
Collegeville, Minnesota

www.litpress.org

A title of the Unitas Books series published by the Liturgical Press

Other titles available in the Unitas Books series:

Justification and the Future of the Ecumenical Movement: The Joint Declaration on the Doctrine of Justification
   William G. Rusch, ed.

I Believe, Despite Everything: Reflections of an Ecumenist
   Jean-Marie R. Tillard

Cover design by McCormick Creative.

The Scripture quotations contained herein are from the New Revised Standard Version Bible, Catholic Edition, copyright © 1989 by the Division of Christian Education of the National Council of the Churches of Christ in the U.S.A., and are used by permission. All rights reserved.

1   2   3   4   5   6   7   8

Library of Congress Cataloging-in-Publication Data

Tjørhom, Ola.
   Visible church, visible unity : ecumenical ecclesiology and "the great tradition of the church" / Ola Tjørhom ; foreword by Geoffrey Wainwright.
      p.   cm.—(Unitas books)
   Includes bibliographical references and index.
   ISBN 0-8146-2873-7 (alk. paper)
   1. Christian union—Lutheran Church.   2. Lutheran Church—Relations—Catholic Church.   3. Christian union—Catholic Church.   4. Catholic Church—Relations—Lutheran Church.   5. Church.   I. Title.   II. Series: Unitas books.

   BX8063.7.C3T55   2004
   262'.72—dc22   2003061074

Unitas Books

On the eve of his crucifixion, Jesus prayed that his followers "may all be one" (John 17:21). Christians believe that this promise is fulfilled in the Church. The Church is Christ's body, and his body cannot be divided. And yet, the churches today live in contradiction to that promise. Churches that recognize in another Christian community an embodiment of the one Church of Jesus Christ still too often find that they cannot live in true communion with them. This contradiction between the Church's unity and its division has driven the ecumenical movement over the last century.

The pursuit of unity will require more than a few mutual adjustments among the Churches. Ecumenism must involve true conversion, a conversion both of hearts and minds, of the will and the intellect. We all must learn to think in new ways about the teachings and practices of the Church. Division has become deeply embedded in the everyday life and thought of the churches. Thinking beyond division will require a new outlook.

Unitas Books seeks to serve the rethinking that is a necessary part of the ecumenical movement. Some books in the series will directly address important topics of ecumenical discussion; others will chart and analyze the ecumenical movement itself. All will be concerned with the Church's unity. Their authors will be ecumenical experts from a variety of Christian traditions, but the books will be written for a wider audience of interested clergy and laypersons. We hope they will be informative for the expert and the newcomer alike.

The unity we seek will be a gift of the Holy Spirit. The Spirit works through means, however, and one of the Spirit's means is careful theological reflection and articulate communication. We hope that this series may be used by the Spirit so that the unity won by Christ may be more fully visible "so that the world may believe" (John 17:21).

Norman A. Hjelm
Michael Root
William G. Rusch

The series editor responsible for this volume is Norman Hjelm.

Contents

Foreword

Geoffrey Wainwright

This book testifies to the agony of an ecumenist at the turn into the twenty-first century. Coming from a Lutheran background, the author has for his historically situated agenda the healing of Western Christendom. Luther's original impulse towards the reformation and renewal of the Western Church has produced mixed results. On the one hand, the Second Vatican Council may be regarded as having met many of Luther's concerns (not before time, one might think; and indulgences can still raise hackles). On the other hand, the history of Luther's project among his own people, as Ola Tjørhom narrates it, is that of a degeneration by successive stages into "Protestantism." Little is said here of the Swiss and English versions of the Reformation, but they too may be assumed to have contributed to, or suffered from, this general decline by way of nationalism *(cuius regio eius religio)*, confessionalism (denominational identity defined over against others), Pietism (here would come, *inter alia,* my own Methodism), and Liberalism (the legacy of the Enlightenment and German Idealism). While the Norwegian interpreter's focus falls most sharply on Europe, his critical analysis of Protestant history bears a striking resemblance to the description of the ecclesiastical and theological scene in North America already offered by the Mercersburg theologian John Williamson Nevin in the middle of the nineteenth century. This "Protestantism" is gnostic in character, marked by rank individualism and a privacy of belief; in "the religious realm," the corporate and the corporeal are spurned. The healing of the divisions in Western Christendom, it is Tjørhom's implicit thesis, can occur only through the healing of the Reformation churches and their reintegration into "the Great Tradition" or "classic Christianity," interpreted and practiced in sacramental key.

Certainly "the Great Tradition of the Church" is the crucial concept in this book. The author describes it thus: (1) it is "grounded in the apostolic witness to Christ as ultimately revealed in Holy Scripture and living on in the church's *anamnesis*"; (2) it is "shaped by the ecumenical creeds of the ancient and undivided church"; (3) it is "fundamentally catholic in the sense that it aims at incorporating the faith of the church in all its richness across time as well as space"; (4) it is "sacramentally, ecclesiologically, and liturgically based, which means that it insists that participation in the fruits of Christ's sacrifice takes place through word and sacrament in the space of the church"; (5) it "realizes that the people of God are a structured people," with pastors providing effective spiritual leadership in its midst and for its benefit; (6) it is convinced that the church is by nature one, its limits defined by heresy; (7) it "holds God's will to be binding and obligatory for human life in its totality," calling for repentance and giving the opportunity for renewal; (8) it gives due weight to the church's "mission and service in the world" as "the priest of creation, as the first-fruit of a reunited humankind, and as a *sacramentum mundi*, a sacrament or sacramental sign in and for the world"; (9) the aim of its mission is "not only that a number of souls be saved, but that God's creation will be redeemed"; (10) it "looks both outward, to the people and the world it is called to serve, and forward to the time of eschatological fulfillment when Christ returns in order to bring his work to completion." Structurally, "the Great Tradition of the Church" is "open to the possibility that visible community on the universal level requires some kind of unity with the Bishop of Rome, the successor of Peter. This should not be perceived as a unity *under* Rome, but as a unity *with* Rome where 'the Western patriarch' has a special responsibility for the church's universal unity within the framework of a comprehensive collegial and synodal structure."

When one tries to read Christian history and the present situation against the standard thus set up, an obvious question arises concerning the relation, theoretical and practical, between Scripture and Tradition. In *Ut Unum Sint*, the 1995 encyclical in which he reaffirms the "irrevocable commitment" of the Roman Catholic Church to ecumenism, John Paul II puts at the top of his list of doctrinal topics needing further study "the relationship between Sacred Scripture, as the highest authority in matters of faith, and Sacred Tradition, as indispensable to the interpretation of the Word of God" (paragraph 79). This strikes me as the most promising for-

mulation of the question since the sixteenth century. The question, however, is not only theoretical but practical. The more one stresses continuity in history, as Tjørhom wishes to, the more it becomes necessary for the
Western churches concretely to evaluate in the light of Scripture the thou-
sand years between, say, St. Augustine or St. Gregory the Great and the
Council of Constance or the Fifth Lateran Council (a task not mentioned
by the author in this book); and not the Middle Ages only, but also the
distinctive histories of both the "Protestant" churches *and* the Roman
Catholic Church in the centuries since the Reformation (perhaps Tjørhom
was both wise and polite to leave the latter initially to Roman Catholics).

In principle, a big ecumenical step was taken at the World Conference on Faith and Order at Montreal in 1963, when Scripture was rec-
ognized as the *internal norm* of the Tradition. It is, of course, only from
within our separated traditions (plural) that we start the process of dis-
cernment; but ecumenical dialogue, through mutual criticism and enrichment, may allow us all to see the truth of the gospel more clearly.

It strikes me that the Joint Declaration on the Doctrine of Justification achieved and ratified in 1998–1999 by the Lutheran World Federation and the Roman Catholic Church provides a positive example of
what may be achieved along the latter lines. A common examination of
the Scriptures and of the respective teachings of the two traditions allowed Lutherans and Catholics to reach exactly the kind of "differentiated consensus" whose character Tjørhom so finely delineates:

> (1) A differentiated consensus embraces both a basic agreement and
> remaining differences. (2) This kind of consensus presupposes a dif-
> ferentiation between church-dividing and non-dividing issues. . . . (3)
> However, [such a] differentiation should not be perceived primarily as a
> perspective on the deposit of faith as a whole, which tends toward a re-
> ductionist distinction between center and periphery. It must rather be
> seen as an approach that must be applied to each "article" or item of
> faith. (4) The building of consensus and its reception should be seen as a
> dialectic between "recognition" and "enrichment" in which we recog-
> nize our faith or the church's faith through the ages in the witness of our
> fellow Christians and at the same time are deeply enriched by the incor-
> poration of new impulses. (5) Ecumenical consensus is definitely not
> only a question of doctrinal agreement; it also aims at a common life that
> includes unity in the celebration of the sacraments, in prayer, structures
> of decision, and in a common mission in and for the world.

It is perhaps strange that Tjørhom does not make more of the exem-
plary character of the Joint Declaration on the Doctrine of Justification;

but he may have been put off by the hostile reaction of so many Protestant theologians in Germany; and of course, even for the supporters of the Joint Declaration, the proof of the pudding will be in the eating, that is, its contribution towards "unity in the celebration of the sacraments, in prayer, structures of decision, and common mission in and for the world." It is imperative that each "differentiated consensus," genuinely achieved, be put to work in favor of fuller unity across the entire range of the lives of the partners.

As I said, the key to "the Great Tradition of the Church" lies for Tjørhom in sacramentality. This is the governing category in his basic ecclesiology (the nature and mission of the Church), his view of ecumenism (the process and achievement of ecclesial unity), and his vision of the Christian life, both individual and communal. Tjørhom cites St. Cyprian's famous dictum that one cannot have God for one's Father without having the Church for one's mother (*On the Unity of the Church*, 6). The Church is the matrix, the palpable locus of salvation; the "hiddenness" of those known only to God is not contradicted by the Church's institutional visibility. This salvific "identity" of the Church is the basis of its mission in and for the world as *sacramentum mundi*. Both the nature and the mission of the Church entail the visibility of its unity: the preaching and hearing of the word; the celebration of the sacraments with word, gesture, and things; a pastoral ministry serving *in persona Christi* in and for the body of Christ. As I myself wrote in *The Ecumenical Moment* (1983): "It is true that verbal and institutional unity would be a mere façade without unity of heart and mind. But spiritual unity and visible unity are not truly alternatives: the alternative to visible unity is visible *dis*unity, and that is a witness against the gospel" (p. 4). And finally, Tjørhom rightly says that a "materialist spirituality" will characterize both the existence of Christians and the life of the Christian community in the world, which has both political and cultural, both social and aesthetic, manifestations.

What, more precisely, about ecumenism? Tjørhom quotes with favor what is indeed the classic description, stemming from the New Delhi Assembly of the World Council of Churches in 1961, of "the unity we seek," "the unity which is both God's will and his gift to his Church." This unity

> is being made visible as all in each place who are baptized into Jesus Christ and confess him as Lord and Saviour are brought by the Holy Spirit into one fully committed fellowship, holding the one apostolic faith, preaching the one Gospel, breaking the one bread, joining in com-

mon prayer, and having a corporate life reaching out in witness and
service to all and who at the same time are united with the whole Christian fellowship in all places and all ages in such wise that ministry and
members are accepted by all, and that all can act and speak together as
occasion requires for the tasks to which God calls his people.

That description was, in fact, drafted almost single-handedly by Bishop
Lesslie Newbigin of the church of South India, who curiously never figures in Tjørhom's book, even though his *Household of God* (1953) and subsequent writings anticipate so much of what Tjørhom's book sets forth.

Tjørhom's book should be heard as a call to the churches to take seriously the New Delhi vision. The years after New Delhi saw various attempts to interpret the vision. Tjørhom views benignly the characteristic
Lutheran notion of "reconciled diversity" as not incompatible with the
"conciliar fellowship" envisaged by the WCC Assembly at Nairobi in
1975, though I myself would certainly regard it as falling short of the "organic unity" that Newbigin, and many others, advocated. Tjørhom himself recognizes that, in Continental European Protestantism, "reconciled
diversity" has degenerated into "static pluralism" or "reconciled denominationalism" (a danger that one might perhaps have detected from the
start). "Reconciled denominationalism" is what Tjørhom calls the 2001
statement of the Evangelical Church in Germany regarding "ein geordnetes Miteinander bekenntnisverschiedener Kirchen"; I might be
tempted to call it, even more rudely, "peaceful coexistence in conditions
of Cold War." Certainly the Leuenberg Concordat and Fellowship (between Lutherans, Reformed, and now Methodists) is inadequate if acqui-
esced in as a goal. Tjørhom may be right in seeing the Porvoo Agreement
between the Anglican churches in Britain and Ireland and most of the
Lutheran churches in Scandinavia and the Baltic as going further in the
transcendence of denominations. But I (and probably he) would recognize that such an arrangement is unlikely to be adequate if the Roman
Catholic and Orthodox Churches were to be part of the picture.

In the North American context, taking seriously the New Delhi vision is precisely what is being asked of the churches and the official
ecumenical agencies by the 2003 Princeton Proposal—"In One Body
through the Cross"—emanating from an informal group of some twenty
leading theologians that includes Orthodox, Catholic, Lutheran, Reformed, Anglican, Methodist, and Pentecostal participants.[1]

---

[1] Carl E. Braaten and Robert W. Jenson, eds., *In One Body through the Cross: The Princeton Proposal for Christian Unity* (Grand Rapids, Mich.: Eerdmans, 2003).

What meanwhile is a committed ecumenist to do? What may he or she hope for and work towards? Where, if anywhere, is one to "go"? Tjørhom himself sees this manifesto of his in terms of a Norwegian saying: "When there is a fire, you don't whisper, you shout!" It is very much a *cri de coeur.* He contemplates three possible courses of action.

The first, following the lines of an evangelical catholicism represented in the early twentieth century by a Nathan Söderblom or a Friedrich Heiler, and later by an Edmund Schlink, a Regin Prenter, an A. C. Piepkorn, would be to stay where one is, and to work within one's own tradition towards a recovery of the Great Tradition or a reentry into it. On the Reformed side, one might think of Jean-Jacques von Allmen and Thomas Torrance; among Methodists, Robert Newton Flew or Albert Outler. That is the line in which I myself have continued.

The second possibility envisaged by Tjørhom is that those "Protestants" with a concern for the Great Tradition should form themselves into communities that not only believe but practice accordingly. This, for Tjørhom, would entail the acquisition of an episcopal ministry in apostolic succession. But can one really in this connection expect help of the kind that Tjørhom discreetly looks for from "especially the Roman Catholic Church and the Orthodox churches" in a positive response to "those who share their faith without being able to become formal members of these churches"? The example of Heiler, who (I think) got himself made a bishop of the *episcopi vagantes* variety, is not very promising. The risk of schism and further fragmentation is great at this point; and it is not unknown for seven worse devils to occupy a vacated place.

The third possibility, according to Tjørhom, is individual or corporate "conversion." Conversion to whom or to what? To Orthodoxy? To Henri de Lubac's *Catholicisme*? Or to the Roman Catholic Church as she empirically is? John Henry Newman's writing of his *Essay on the Development of Christian Doctrine* took him to the Roman Catholic Church (or justified the step to which he was already intuitively committed) as the best embodiment of original and continuingly authentic Christianity. Jaroslav Pelikan's pilgrimage led him to the Orthodox Church in America. It seems that Ola Tjørhom has now decided to follow Newman. I wish him well. Others may judge that the *mutual* correction and enrichment for which all ecumenists hope requires a more patient working and waiting until a significant proportion of one's own community, if not indeed the whole of it, is ready. Even the Protestant traditions have blessings to contribute, diachronically and synchronically, to the Great Tradition.

We may be in for some surprises. Tjørhom himself ascribes a vital role to pneumatology in the Great Tradition and in the ecumenical movement. A remarkable sign in recent decades is the dialogue between the Roman Catholic Church and "some classical Pentecostals." Then there are the international conferences on the Holy Spirit and Christian unity sponsored by the Cardinal Suenens Center at John Carroll University under the direction of Doris Donnelly. Are we already on the verge of "The Next Christendom" forecast by Philip Jenkins in his 2001 book under that title? Given the southward shift in Christianity's demographic center of gravity, I had expressed the hope, in *The Ecumenical Moment*, that the Western churches might put their own house in order before handing on their historic responsibilities to the churches of the South. Time presses; that moment may be gone. We must certainly pray that "the next Christendom" will, by grace, remain committed to the Great Tradition of a christocentric trinitarian faith and its visible embodiment in ecclesial life.

The Divinity School
Duke University
Durham, North Carolina
Epiphany 2003

Preface

When I was asked to prepare this volume for *Unitas Books*, the intention was to present a contribution toward an ecumenical ecclesiology, that is, a reflection on the Church that would make sense to faithful from different ecclesial traditions and that would draw on and contribute to the ongoing ecumenical dialogue on this crucial topic. This contribution would be anchored primarily in "the Great Tradition of the Church." It was also foreseen that I could base my work on my Norwegian volume on the same topic, a volume that has been used as textbook for theological students in all Scandinavian countries, *Kirken—troens mor: Et økumenisk bidrag til en luthersk ekklesiologi*, "The Church—Mother of Faith: An Ecumenical Contribution to a Lutheran Ecclesiology" (Oslo: Verbum, 1999).

However, as the present work developed, I felt a need to widen its scope, since it became increasingly clear to me that I had to start with a critical evaluation of the ecclesiological reflections and practices of my own Lutheran tradition. It seemed particularly important to make an assessment of post-Reformation developments. This was not, to be sure, a new concern to me. During the three years I served as research professor at the Institute for Ecumenical Research in Strasbourg, both the vast distance between the original ecclesiology of the Lutheran Reformers and the currently dominating attitudes at this point (in "Protestant" camouflage) and the vacuum that seems to mark Lutheran reflection in this field today convinced me that radical and substantial changes are required. Some may find my critical assessment biased and exaggerated, but as the late Norwegian writer Alexander Kielland insisted, "When there is a fire, you don't whisper—you shout!"

Parallel to this, a personal development has also set its mark on the present volume: I came to feel more and more foreign to, or even homeless in, my own church. Not that my theology has changed much over the last fifteen to twenty years; I am still, and assume that I will in a sense always remain, an "evangelical catholic." But both my Strasbourg experiences and the present state of the Church of Norway have made me realize that what I see as the authentic catholicity and ecumenicity of the Reformation movement is being transformed by a massive "Protestantization," a phenomenon that I describe as "liberal-pietism." Simultaneously, a rapid and radical marginalization of evangelical catholicity has taken place in most Lutheran churches, particularly on the European continent.

Let me make a long story short. This development and the rather painful feeling of being homeless in what is meant to be our home in this world have led to a decision to convert. When this volume is published, I shall, *Deo volente,* be a member of the Roman Catholic Church. People have chosen this path for different reasons. Some convert to a cultural-aesthetic program—or to Graham Greene. For me this was different; I simply converted to Catholicism. And I did so because I found it increasingly difficult to live out my Catholic faith in a Lutheran setting. In more concrete terms, my conversion depends largely on the conviction that today the Roman Catholic Church is the best, if not necessarily the only, place to fulfill the original intention of the Reformation in general and of authentic Lutheran ecclesiology in particular.

I hope that this paradoxical view will become somewhat less so in the following chapters of this book. This is not meant to imply that my book should be read as a conversion narrative. It was, however, written during a time when my wish to seek communion with the Roman Catholic Church matured and became a firm resolution. This fact may help explain possible tensions or theological inconsistencies in the following account, simply because the manuscript was produced in a period of transition from one church to another. What I write may be neither Lutheran nor entirely Catholic. Yet my key intention to contribute to an ecumenical ecclesiology on the basis of "the Great Tradition" remains unchanged.

Like an ellipsis, this volume has a double center or focus: ecclesiology and ecumenism. This reflects my conviction that unity belongs inseparably and necessarily to the church's nature. These two centers of my theological ellipsis will be further developed in five chapters. These chapters deal with several issues: the original intention of the

Reformers and the present state of the Reformation project; the "Great Tradition of the Church" as a feasible way forward, not a nostalgic dead end; the Church as the place of salvation and the consequent necessity of a sacramentally anchored ecclesiology; our increasingly vague commitment to the goal of visible unity and the need to reaffirm this commitment; and what I describe as a "materialist spirituality," also a vital part of ecclesiology.

Admittedly, my enterprise is limited, since I cannot claim to be fully informed about current developments in all parts of the Protestant world. However, even if this account is based largely on the situation in European Lutheranism, there are presumably so many features common to—especially—the North American situation that I dare to hope that my approach will be relevant to readers beyond Europe. To be sure, there are other topics that could also have been discussed here, but I have focused on the ones I consider most pertinent. Moreover, even if both the format of *Unitas Books* and the limited time at my disposal have forced me to keep my reflections rather brief, occasionally forcing me into an almost compendium-like style, it remains my hope that I have been able to present an integral picture of the Church in this work. Finally, when I offer this contribution to an ecumenical ecclesiology, my aim is not to present something that will be easy to swallow in all camps and within all traditions. Even if catholicity requires comprehensiveness and generosity, these concepts are not identical. The key concern behind an ecumenical way of doing ecclesiology is rather to break away from narrow denominational and parochial views that are not even remotely able to reflect the vast richness of the Church.

I would like to express my appreciation to those who have made this project possible. This includes a deep gratitude to the editors of *Unitas Books* for asking me to write this book. I am particularly grateful to Norman Hjelm for his valuable help in editing the manuscript. Also, I must thank the faculty at the School of Mission and Theology in Stavanger, Norway, for letting me sit down for some months in peace and quiet after my return from Strasbourg in order to finish this volume.

As indicated above, three aspects are central to the present venture: critical, constructive, and personal. However, these aspects are kept together by a fundamental common denominator, namely, my wish to emphasize the basic visibility of the Church and ecclesial life. On a critical level, I would argue that "liberal-pietism" and Protestant Lutheranism have ended up with a perception of the Church as a vague idea or an abstract entity that neither is nor has a body. In a more constructive perspective, my main concern is to make it clear that the church and its unity are just as empirically recognizable as the external word and the concrete sacraments that constitute it, and at the same time make it clear that there is a "physical" character or anchoring of our life in Christ that follows from this visibility.

However, during the process that ended up with my decision to convert to Roman Catholicism, I realized that the visibility of the Church also played a vital role in this connection. This is reflected by an incident that occurred in a conversation on prayer with a Catholic priest when I was in catechesis. "I have to admit that my prayer life is rather miserable, Father," I muttered. "Is that so, my son?" he replied. "We'll have to look into that." "Well, I find it increasingly difficult to concentrate." "But you can see?" Still being somewhat immersed in Protestant piety, I thought he was asking for some kind of inner spiritual vision, which I had to admit that I hadn't had for a long time. "No, my son, you got me all wrong. The question isn't if you have a vision, but simply if your eyes function properly." "I assume they do," I answered with a certain amount of puzzlement. "Then start coming to our sacramental devotions following Mass every Thursday. And keep your eyes fixed on the Blessed Sacrament. Such 'gazing' is also a kind of prayer." After some Thursdays I realized that the padre was right—gazing can actually be praying too.

In my opinion, this incident reflects why the visibility of the Church and its unity is so crucial. What is at stake is definitely not an isolated concern for grand hierarchies and massive structures. The point is simply that faith never sits exclusively in our hearts or minds, let alone in abstract ideas; faith also exists in our concrete empirical perceptions. And in the present time, when our lives are becoming increasingly hectic and our minds increasingly dispersed, such an awareness is particularly important. This is the basic lesson of the Holy Eucharist: through the basic acts of eating and drinking, we become one with Christ. Fortunately, I can see, in the same way that I can hear, smell, and taste. Moreover, when my senses are weakened, I pray that God will sustain my memory of what I have seen, heard, and tasted. This is the gospel of the empirical perceptibility of grace. And surely a church that carries and witnesses to this mystery cannot be essentially invisible.

Ola Tjørhom
Stavangar, Norway
Epiphany, 2003

Chapter 1

Toward the End of the Reformation Project? The Riddle of Protestantism

The Lutheran Reformation started as a renewal movement within the one Catholic Church. Since this "renewal" has now been going on for almost five hundred years, it is pertinent to ask some critical questions about the Reformation project and its future: Do the Reformation churches still possess the required potential for renewal? Or are several of the original concerns of the Reformers in danger of vanishing within today's Lutheran churches? How long does it actually make sense to cling to a self-understanding as "a renewal movement" when this movement has increasingly taken the shape of a denominational institution? These questions are vital, for a renewal movement that stops asking them immediately puts its very capacity for renewal in jeopardy. And further, the claim of "continual reformation" is surely not only relevant externally but also internally.

In this chapter I shall try to address this challenge with a special view to the future of the Reformation project. My main aim is to convey concerns that are essential in regard to current efforts both to evaluate the Lutheran Reformation and to identify tasks and prospects that lie ahead. The following picture is, to be sure, personal, yet I would like to underscore my genuine concern for the original identity and authenticity of the Reformation movement, even if I do find it increasingly difficult to identify with today's version of the movement.

This particularly applies to Protestantism, which is a great riddle to me (to allude to Jaroslav Pelikan's famous book of 1960, *The Riddle of Roman Catholicism*). Admittedly, Lutheranism and Protestantism are not identical entities. But a notable "Protestantization" has clearly come to mark significant parts of the Reformation movement, a development that I regard as a most serious threat to authentic Reformation theology in general and to the ecclesiology of the Reformers in particular. I shall explore this view further, but initially I would like to underline that the concept "Protestantism" is here used more to picture a historical post-Reformation development on the European continent that has its main roots in the nineteenth century than as a description of existing churches. My point is clearly not to collectively dismiss all churches that see themselves as Protestant.

The Original Intention of the Lutheran Reformation

Martin Luther is often seen as a heroic figure who fought uncompromisingly against "the Papists." Moreover, he is frequently pictured as an early representative of modernity who defended personal liberty over against the church institution. And he is also described as someone who produced completely new thoughts, vehemently rejected traditionalism, and, so to speak, reinvented religion. In this way Luther becomes an individual rebel who escaped ecclesial dictatorship as well as the limitations of the past. This understanding of Luther dominates what can be called "Reformation hagiography," propagated by certain Luther research initiatives that are both devoid of critical perspective and ecumenically counterproductive. Thus Luther—a densely Protestant Luther—is carved in the image of nineteenth-century Protestantism and is given an infallibility of which hardly any pope can dream.

However, such a picture is both historically and theologically deceptive. Martin Luther cannot be described solely as an anti-Catholic rebel. Quite to the contrary, he saw himself as a good Catholic—in many ways as a significantly *better* Catholic than many leaders in his church. And his original intention was not in any sense to establish a new church, but rather to contribute to a renewal of the *una sancta* that has Christ as its cornerstone and the apostles as its foundation. Luther was firmly convinced that this, and not some kind of religious fringe group, was the church to which he belonged. This is also the reason why he affirmed that "there is much truly Christian and good under the papacy—as a matter of fact all that is truly Christian and good has come to us from this source."[1]

---

[1] Quoted from *Von der Wiedertaufe* of 1528; see Weimar Ausgabe (WA), *Martin Luthers Werke, Kritische Ausgabe*, 26, 147. Concerning Martin Luther and his catholicity in general, see also David Yeago, "The Catholic Luther," *First Things,* no. 61 (March 1996) 37ff.

Despite a certain ambiguity, this aspect is even more clearly expressed by the so-called Melanchthonian tradition propagated by Luther's main collaborator, Philipp Melanchthon, and reflected in clearly the most important Lutheran confessional writing, the Augsburg Confession (AC) of 1530.[2] In its preface the *Confessio Augustana* affirms that both parties at the Diet of Augsburg "exist and fight under one Christ, so we may also be able to live in one Christian church in unity and concord. "[3] Moreover, in the conclusion of the first part of the Augsburg Confession, the Reformers explicitly state that there is "nothing here [in their doctrine] that departs from the catholic church or from the Roman church" *(ab ecclesia catholica vel ab ecclesia Romana)*. Seen in this perspective, there is ample reason to speak about the catholicity and ecumenicity of the Reformation, at least in regard to its authentic goal and in its initial stages.

This catholicity and ecumenicity are often perceived to be a consequence of Melanchthon's *"Leisetreterei,"* his allegedly somewhat careful or even timid approach. However, in several of the central Reformation writings a basic catholicity and ecumenicity emerge as a crucial theological concern and not only as a tactically or practically motivated position. This is clearly the case in the Augsburg Confession, which, for example, insists in Article V, "Concerning Ministry in the Church," that we participate in the fruits of Christ's sacrificial offering through the means of grace as administered in the space of the church by its ordained ministry, clearly a fundamental Catholic concern. Moreover, in AC Article XIV, "Concerning Church Order," the Reformers virtually quote from then current canonical laws in insisting

---

[2] On the basic catholicity and catholic contents of the Augsburg Confession, see Harding Meyer and Heinz Schütte, eds., *Confessio Augustana: Bekenntnis des einen Glaubens. Gemeinsame Untersuchung lutherischer und katholischer Theologen* (Paderborn: Bonifatius-Verlag; Frankfurt am Main: Otto Lembeck, 1980), as well as "All Under One Christ: Statement on the Augsburg Confession by the Roman Catholic/Lutheran Joint Commission," in Harding Meyer and Lukas Vischer, eds., *Growth in Agreement: Reports and Agreed Statements of Ecumenical Conversations on a World Level* (New York: Paulist Press; Geneva: World Council of Churches, 1984) 241–247; see also Joseph A. Burgess, ed., *The Role of the Augsburg Confession: Catholic and Lutheran Views* (Philadelphia: Fortress Press, 1980). For a good introduction to Melanchthon and his theology, see Heinz Scheible, *Melanchthon: Eine Biographie* (Munich: C. H. Beck, 1997). Generally, evidences of theological ambiguity in Melanchthon are often associated with his less gratifying positions on the Real Presence and the doctrine of justification.

[3] Most quotations from the Lutheran Confessions here are taken from Robert Kolb and Timothy J. Wengert, eds., *The Book of Concord: The Confessions of the Evangelical Lutheran Church* (Minneapolis: Fortress Press, 2000).

that only those who are "properly called" *(rite vocatus)*, or ordained to the public ministry of the church, shall be allowed to administer word and sacraments. Similar concerns are expressed in Melanchthon's Apology of the Augsburg Confession, for instance when he characterizes the ordained ministry as a representation of Christ (Apol. VII) and affirms that ordination can be described as a sacrament or a sacramental act (Apol. XIII). Generally the key concern of the Reformers, as expressed in the conclusion of the first part of the Augsburg Confession, was to correct certain abuses that had penetrated the Church. There is much evidence that if largely practical abuses, such as the laity being given only the bread at the Eucharist, the prohibition of marriage for priests, and so-called private Masses, had been adjusted, the emerging division could have been avoided.[4]

Three central features that marked the intention of the Reformers are vital to our interpretation of their message. (1) The Lutheran Reformation possessed a catholic intention and an ecumenical commitment. This is reflected in the Reformers' affirmation of what they saw as authentic catholicity in accordance with Holy Scripture and the witness of the early Church, as well as in their emphasis on the need to preserve unity. (2) The Reformation understood itself as a renewal movement within the one church. Lutheranism should not be perceived as a separate church institution or denomination of perpetual legitimacy. In point of fact, this renewal movement is continually to aim at making itself redundant. In any case, its raison d'être and continued existence depend heavily on its actual potential for renewal. (3) Authentic Reformation thought should not be seen first and foremost as a conscious attempt to develop a complete theological system, but rather as a "regulative" or "reactive" effort focused on areas in which the prevailing Roman Catholic doctrine and practice were seen as lacking or erroneous. Accordingly, the "Great Catholic Tradition" emerges as the most appropriate, perhaps even the only possible, interpretative framework of the Lutheran Reformation. And when this framework is missing or neglected, a correct understanding of the Reformers' message will not be possible.

---

[4] For a more comprehensive discussion of the "catholic nature" of the Reformation and its ecumenical implication, see Carl E. Braaten, "Die Katholizität der Reformation: Der Ort der Reformation in der Bewegung der Evangelischen Katholiken," *Kerygma und Dogma* 42 (1996) 186ff.; Carl E. Braaten and Robert W. Jenson, eds., *The Catholicity of the Reformation* (Grand Rapids, Mich.: Eerdmans, 1996).

The Post-Reformation Development—Continuous Decay?

It is not possible here to discuss in detail the development of the Lutheran Reformation.[5] However, in light of the picture that has been presented here, there is in my view much in evidence that this development in its main features must be characterized as a continual deviation from the authentic roots and shape of the Reformation. This process actually started fairly soon after the Diet of Augsburg in 1530. It accelerated when growing political contradictions set their definite mark on the Reformation movement in connection with the Schmalkald War and the Peace of Augsburg in 1555, with its insistence on the *cuius regio eius religio* principle, a principle that implied that the sovereign was to decide the religion of the people. And it becomes an unavoidable theological fact through Pietism and the so-called liberal theology of the late nineteenth and early twentieth centuries. Among several features that mark this development, the following three play a particularly crucial and fateful role:

1. *The political undergirding and consolidation of the Reformation.* Basically, the ecclesiastical discord of the early sixteenth century was itself part of a comprehensive political struggle. In confrontation with the allied pope and emperor, the evangelical congregations could survive only within the framework of a political union with the German nobility. However, this politicizing had significant theological repercussions, since the princes were given a key role in church governance, even exercising certain episcopal functions. And when an evangelical state-church system was developed in the wake of the *cuius regio eius religio* principle, whatever theological differences that might have

---

[5] Concerning literature on the Post-Reformation development and its roots, see Eamon Duffy, *The Stripping of the Altars: Traditional Religion in England 1400–1580* (New Haven: Yale University Press, 1992). This work is a vital corrective to common Protestant interpretations of the time of the Reformation in general and in particular to their insistence that the Roman Catholic Church of that time was marked by massive decay and little else. On the Post-Reformation development, see Joseph Lortz, *Die Reformation in Deutschland,* 2 vols. (Freiburg: Herder, 1939–1940); Heiko A. Oberman, *The Impact of the Reformation* (Grand Rapids, Mich.: Eerdmans, 1994); Thomas Kaufmann, "Die Konfessionalisierung von Kirche und Gesellschaft," *Theologische Literaturzeitung* 121 (1996) cols. 1008ff. and 1112ff. With regard to even later developments, see Walter von Loewenich, *Luther und der Neuprotestantismus* (Witten: Kreuz, 1963); Horst Stephan and Martin Schmidt, *Geschichte der evangelischen Theologie in Deutschland seit dem Idealismus,* 3rd ed. (Berlin and New York: De Gruyter, 1973); Wolfhart Pannenberg, *Problemgeschichte der neueren evangelischen Theologie in Deutschland* (Göttingen: Vandenhoeck & Ruprecht, 1979); Helmut Thielicke, *Glauben und Denken in der Neuzeit: Die grossen Systeme der Theologie und Religionsphilosophie* (Tübingen: J.C.B. Mohr [Paul Siebeck], 1983).

existed were given a kind of political superstructure that made them even more insurmountable. Seen in this perspective, it may be argued that the emerging ecclesial divisions were not due solely to unsolved theological questions but just as much to massive European political contradictions between regional structures and central powers like pope and emperor. In any case, the institution of the state-church system implied that the ecumenicity of the Reformation was severely restricted; for instance, in Denmark/Norway only Lutherans could be full citizens. Moreover, this system also contributed significantly to a densely pragmatic ecclesiology.

2. *The "confessionalization" or "denominationalization" of Reformation theology.* The mid-sixteenth-century church division led to a perhaps not totally conscious but nevertheless notable shift regarding the basic theological intention of the Reformation. Instead of wishing to contribute to renewal within the one church, the felt need to establish a comprehensive theological system for a particular church body came to play an increasingly crucial role. Hence the authentic catholicity and ecumenicity of the Reformation movement was gradually weakened by, or even exchanged for, a growing emphasis on confessional or denominational identity. This development gained pace when politically conditioned divisions were in effect. Its result was that the Reformation renewal movement was turned into a "denomination" with increasing parochial features. And as things developed, this denominational concern was directed more and more against the Roman Catholic Church and thus against catholicism.

3. *A "theologization" of what the Reformers saw as contextually governed emergency solutions.* This was particularly visible as regards ecclesiology. Here the break in the historic episcopal succession in large parts of the Reformation movement comes through as a key example. When Luther's collaborator Johannes Bugenhagen, who was not ordained as a bishop, was commissioned to install so-called superintendents in Denmark and subsequently also in Norway and Iceland, the key aim was to cope with the need of evangelical congregations for episcopal oversight. In a situation where such oversight was denied to them by the Roman Catholic authorities, alternative approaches had to be found. However, these approaches were not understood to be permanent, and definitely not as conscious or explicit breaks with the *successio apostolica.* Accordingly, it is totally misleading when this kind of contextually conditioned emergency measures later on have become a kind of perpetual theological concern that largely canonizes them as

fundamental components of the Reformation heritage and identity. This was never the case with the Reformers, who were firmly committed to keep the episcopal order or polity of the Church.

As already indicated, this movement away from original Reformation positions took the Pietism of the late seventeenth and early eighteenth centuries, together with the liberal theology that took shape in the nineteenth and early twentieth centuries, for its decisive theological foundation. Both these currents correspond to the emerging anthropocentrism of the sixteenth century as well as the Kantian criticism of the eighteenth century, particularly in light of the latter's break with an ontologically directed theology based on creation or with theological reflection that aims at saying something about being and the world as they really are. Later on Kantian impulses were turned into a more conscious theological system by Friedrich Schleiermacher and his insistence that religion is *Gefühl*, "feeling." Pietism as well as liberalism is marked by a general "anthropologization" of theology by grounding religion more or less exclusively in the human being, in our "hearts," as the Pietists preferred, or in our "souls," the favored liberal solution. What is more, these two currents stand out as largely anti-ecclesiological and anti-sacramental. Here the church institution was seen at best as a purely practical framework for personal belief, at worst as a significant impediment to authentic religiosity.

And lastly, both Pietism and liberalism were marked by theological minimalism or reductionism. This was particularly the case in regard to the interpretation of the Lutheran Reformation principles of Scripture alone, faith alone, and grace alone. These principles were by and large understood as in themselves sufficient, and so largely as isolated theological concepts and not as efforts to identify a hermeneutical core for the rich universe of Christian faith and tradition. Obviously, there are many significant differences between pietistic and liberal approaches. However, particularly when these entities are seen in an ecclesiological perspective, they emerge as two of a kind. There seems to be ample reason to speak of a kind of "liberal-pietistic alliance," an alliance that provides the basis for contemporary Protestantism and has proved also to be highly influential in churches today.[6]

---

[6] This interpretation draws heavily on a publication by one of my teachers in Oslo, Leiv Aalen, *Testimonium Spiritus Sancti som teologisk "prinsipp"* (Oslo: Lutherstiftelsen, 1938); see also his doctoral dissertation on Nikolaus Zinzendorf, *Den unge Zinzendorfs teologi* (Oslo: Lutherstiftelsen, 1952). Regrettably, these books are available only in Norwegian.

Looking at the situation of the Reformation churches in the twenty-first century, it must be admitted that it is difficult to present an accurate evaluation. This is due to the fact that such an account will unavoidably be colored by personal likes and dislikes, but, even more, a vast, often confusing plurality appears to be one of the key marks of contemporary Lutheranism. However, let me, in spite of these difficulties, try to briefly identify some factors that contribute to at least significant parts of the Reformation movement in its liberal-pietistic disguise today.

1) Old confessionalist attitudes marked by anti-catholic tendencies seem to have been revived lately. This is the case with regard to the "WordAlone" movement in the United States as well as within traditionally "liberal" Evangelical churches on the European continent. Here care for confessional identity emerges as a divisive factor of a sub-theological kind and not as a gift that we are committed to share with others within a living communion. Moreover, anti-catholic attitudes serve as a link between conservatism and liberalism.

2) The ongoing doctrinal disintegration of Lutheranism has led to the fact that the distinction in AC Article VII between what is sufficient *(satis)* for true church fellowship and what is not necessary *(nec necesse)* is frequently turned upside down: In an attempt to compensate for radical doctrinal pluralism, there emerges a proclivity toward uniformism with regard to order and structure that is particularly directed toward "Catholic remnants" in the Lutheran churches.

3) Continuity in worship life and especially the celebration of the eucharist is threatened by an apparently irresistible urge to reinvent the wheel. Cardinal Newman's rather gloomy prediction that "To be deep in history is to cease to be a Protestant" (*Essay on the Development of Christian Doctrine,* intro., sect. 5) seems to be affirmed as a reality that also prevents our liturgies from serving as a firm point and a link of continuity.

4) Theological reflection has been turned into a kind of acrobatics with abstract principles that are neither anchored in the church nor in the lives of human beings. This is particularly the case as regards an understanding of the doctrine of justification, in which justification before God is dissociated from its sacramental basis and its ecclesial framework as well as its fundamental grounding in Christ and his work. One is left with the impression that it is "the doctrine of justification" that justifies and not Christ himself.

5) Repeated concession to private preferences (people believe, but in their own way) and to a kind of market religiosity (we pick and choose whatever appeals to us from a vast religious cafeteria) have

contributed effectively to the ongoing disintegration of Lutheranism. Obviously, such attitudes leave little room for the exercise of authority in the life of the Church. Today bishops are expected to function more as administrators of pluralism than as effective signs of unity and continuity with the task of teaching authoritatively.

At this point I would like to add an observation on the present status of ecclesiology within the Church of Norway. As far as I can see, the adherence to a privatized and half secularized pietism, or rather liberal-pietism, in combination with a folk-church ideology and a state-church system has proved to be particularly destructive in regard to ecclesiological reflection. We have already noticed that liberal-pietism has no need for the Church in its accommodation to people's demand to freely construct their own private religiosity. The folk-church idea, today emerging as the chief operative dogma of the Church of Norway and even being explicitly affirmed in its recent church laws, points toward a highly static ecclesiology. Admittedly, the Church should and must be seen as a folk church in view of its mission commitment, but this principle is not even remotely sufficient when it comes to efforts to account for the Church's nature and identity. In recent Norwegian debates, the present principle has paved the way for a quite remarkable ecclesiological timidity in which the reflections on the Church and its practice are governed by a paralyzing fear to say or do anything that may upset the *populus*. Moreover, the state-church system requires and promotes an ecclesiological pragmatism that has taken an almost self-destructive form.[7] All these factors have led to the fact that the ecclesiological vacuum that marks post-Reformation Protestantism has become particularly distinct within the Church of Norway.

In an often highly accurate picture of the ongoing disintegration of the mainline churches and their more or less "collapsing institutions," David Mills underlines the following features.[8] First, at least in

---

[7] On the Norwegian state-church system in ecclesiological perspective, see Ola Tjørhom, "Same Church—New Order: A Report on Church-State Relations in Norway and Its Ecclesiological Implications," *Pro Ecclesia*, vol. 11, no. 3 (2002) 261ff. In addition to offering a striking example of the ecclesiological vacuum of Protestantism and its static perception of the Church, the report in question also reflects and advocates the strange Protestant idea that one can change the Church's "order" while keeping its "essence" unchanged.

[8] See David Mills, *A Hope for Collapsing Churches: The Inevitable Decline of the Mainline Churches and the Renewal of the Church,* found on the web page of Trinity Episcopal School for Ministry, but originally published in *The Evangelical Catholic*. On the so-called "Lat-Cons," see David Mills, "Meet the LatCons," *Touchstone* (Winter 1996).

the initial stages, these institutions "simply deny the problems," often by appealing to a rhetoric of "unity in diversity." Second, "institutions that have lost their shared beliefs begin to centralize," in the sense that organizational unity is given priority over lost unity in faith. Third, centralization is followed by a massive homogenization that is directed particularly against "extremes" and "eccentrics." Fourth, as a compensation for lost unity in faith, collapsing institutions initiate a "frantic invention of programs, projects and 'vision statements'" in order to try to create "some sort of unity. " Fifth and finally, "'divisive' members" are expelled, directly or indirectly, in the hope that "their leaving might restore the lost unity." These attitudes are militantly supported by liberals, effectively propagated by an increasingly more technocrat church leadership, and even implicitly sustained by so-called "Latitudinarian conservatives" (LatCons), who tend to prioritize vague harmony and not the truth. Without necessarily agreeing with all parts of Mills's account, it is difficult to deny that the picture he presents fits quite well with the developments that are taking place among European and American Lutherans.

Let me try to summarize my interpretation of the post-Reformation development. At first, the former catholic and ecumenical renewal movement was politicized; then it was denominational—and then Protestant. Today the large Lutheran churches, at least in Europe but probably also in North America, often come across as embracing almost everything, and thus as having no clear profile whatsoever. Clearly, contemporary "liberal-pietism" is radically shaped by postmodern pluralism. All in all, the Reformation movement finds itself at a vast distance from its roots. And this distance grows continually, almost to the point where we are forced to talk about a completely *new* movement that has lost touch with the catholic intention and ecumenical commitment of the Reformers. As we shall see, this is particularly the case in the field of ecclesiology.

The Protestant Threat to Reformation Ecclesiology

The ecclesiological deliberations of the Reformers in general and Martin Luther in particular are marked by a certain discrepancy.[9] On

---

[9] It is striking to have to register that an old publication like Ernst Kinder, *Der evangelische Glaube und die Kirche. Grundzüge des evangelischen Kirchenverständnisses* (Berlin: Lutherisches Verlagshaus, 1958), remains one of the few available ecclesiologies written

the one hand, these deliberations contain concerns of lasting importance. This is primarily the case with regard to the insistence that the Church is constituted by the means of grace as these means are administered in worship. Accordingly, Reformation ecclesiology is marked by a strong focus on word, sacraments, and worship. This is reflected in AC Article VII with its affirmation that the "pure" preaching of the gospel and the "right" administration of the sacraments are the main criteria of true church unity. But ecclesiologically speaking, it is manifested in an even more convincing way in the insistence of Article V that we participate in the justifying fruits of Christ's unique sacrificial offering through the means of grace as these means are mediated to us in the Church through the service of the ordained ministry. Luther's strong criticism of the so-called radical Reformers for turning God's ordinance upside down by placing his "inward" work in our hearts before his "outward" work through the means of grace is most significant. This criticism is based on its crucial pneumatological implications, its stress on the Holy Spirit's working through outwardly or empirically recognizable means, and thus rejection of falsely "spiritualized" understandings. Finally, the perception of the ordained ministry as a service in the midst of, as well as over against, the faithful and as a fundamental instrument of salvation through its role in the mediation of word and sacrament comes through as a vital ecclesiological concern of the Reformation.

Simultaneously, it must be acknowledged that what has been said earlier about the regulative or reactive character of Reformation theology definitely applies also to its ecclesiology. This means that efforts to identify a "complete" Reformation ecclesiology are in vain, since the Reformers never developed a full ecclesiological system of their own. Here we are facing two types of deliberations: viewpoints that confirm that the Reformers stand safely in the church's true tradition and do not represent some marginal sect, and viewpoints that emphasize what was seen as particularly problematic in the teaching and practice of the Roman Catholic Church. Accordingly, it cannot be denied that Reformation ecclesiology is marked by a stern criticism of several aspects of the Roman

---

from a Lutheran perspective that are really worth reading. But see also Gordon W. Lathrop, *Holy People: A Liturgical Ecclesiology* (Minneapolis: Fortress Press, 1999), and Ola Tjørhom, *Kirken—troens mor: Et økumenisk bidrag til en luthersk ekklesiologi* (Oslo: Verbum, 1999). Within contemporary Protestantism, there is a huge amount of what we may label as "church and " literature, but notably few theological ecclesiologies.

Catholic position, often focusing primarily on practical-theological factors. At the same time, the Reformers' understanding of the Church was
based on Holy Scripture, further developed and adapted by the early
Church, and, despite all deviations and problems, handed over through
the centuries within the Roman Catholic Church. All in all, this indicates
that Reformation ecclesiology can hardly be understood properly when
its Catholic foundation is played down or neglected.

However, this is exactly what has happened within Protestantism. Let me try to substantiate this by indicating some examples of a
significant ecclesiological shift in post-Reformation developments.
(1) While the Reformers always remained convinced that the Church and
the sacraments are fundamental to the mediation of salvation, we have
already noted that liberal-pietists tend to see these entities as an impediment to authentic personal religiosity.[10] (2) Protestants confuse the
Reformers' strong view that the Church can be hidden (*verborgen*) with
an essential invisibility. Accordingly, they neglect the fact that while
Luther as well as AC Article VIII may describe the true church (*ecclesia
proprie dicta*) as hidden with regard to its real members, the same
church is presented as just as visible or "audible" as the outward word
and the empirically recognizable sacraments that constitute it. (3) Protestants tend to read the *satis est* of AC Article VII as a prohibition
against attributing ecclesiological significance to factors in the Church's
life other than word and sacrament. However, by such an ecclesiological minimalism the fact is overlooked that the ministry of the Church,
in the light of AC Article V, with its stress on the role of the ordained
ministry in the administration of the means of grace, can by implication be seen as church constitutive; overlooked also is the plain fact
that Martin Luther in his writings lists respectively seven and eleven
empirical marks (*notae*) of the Church.[11] Generally, I would argue that
AC Article V is more important to, and representative of, Reformation
ecclesiology than AC Article VII. For while the Augsburg Confession

---

[10] A more recent example of a typically Protestant downplaying of ecclesiology can
be found in Leif Grane, "Die ekklesiologische Bedeutung der Rechtfertigungslehre aus
Luthers Sicht," *Zeitschrift für Theologie und Kirche* 10 (December 1998) 1ff. In Grane's interpretation, the appropriate grounding of ecclesiology in the doctrine of justification
seems to point toward a clearly less appropriate insistence that there is no ecclesiology.

[11] See here respectively *On the Councils and the Church* of 1539 and *Against Hanswurst*
of 1541, both of which are found in *Luther's Works* 41 (Philadelphia: Fortress Press, 1966).
What is, in my opinion, a counterproductive interpretation of the *satis est* of AC Article
VII can be found in James Kittelson, "Enough Is Enough! The Confusion over the Augsburg Confession and Its Satis Est," *Lutheran Quarterly* 12 (1998) 279ff.

deals with the nature and essential role of the Church, the *(satis est)* of AC Article VII should rather be seen as an effort to locate a practical *modus vivendi* over against the institution of the Roman Catholic Church and not as a the core of a complete ecclesiology.

Let me make mention of two additional examples of the shift that has taken place within post-Reformation Protestantism in the area of sacramental and ministerial theology. While the Real Presence and its concrete implications were absolutely crucial to Martin Luther's understanding of the Eucharist, this concern is often reduced among contemporary Lutherans to an abstract principle, to something which may be attributed with a general importance as a theological "idea," but which is largely invisible in the way the Lord's Supper is celebrated. It is important to recall that Luther excommunicated two priests, Wolferinus and Besserer, for defending and practicing what the vast majority of today's Lutheran pastors do every time they celebrate the Eucharist: putting consecrated bread back in the box together with unconsecrated bread as if nothing had happened to it. To Luther, such an attitude and practice put the Real Presence in jeopardy.[12] Moreover, the Lutheran emphasis on the appropriate application of the elements (cf. the *in usu* principle) must primarily be understood as a reminder that the eucharistic elements should be used as intended—that is, consumed—and not as a limitation of the sacramental presence.

Turning to the theology of the ministry, we have another example. In this regard, the most obvious shift within Protestantism is that the ordained ministry of the Church is mixed together with the so-called common priesthood, "the priesthood of all believers," or better, the priesthood of the baptized faithful. Both are essential to the Church's life, but they tend to lose their positive meaning when they are seen as competing entities on the same level. For while the priesthood of the faithful is a participation in Christ's priesthood—implying that we can approach God without mediators like the high priest of the Old

---

[12] Besserer lost some of the consecrated bread during a eucharistic celebration. He then distributed an unconsecrated host, and when he found the lost bread, he put it back with the unconsecrated bread. Wolferinus, pastor in Eisleben, Luther's birthplace, defended theologically and in practice the view that the Real Presence only applied to the *actio sacramentalis*. On Luther's initiative and after much commotion, both these "Zwinglian" cases resulted in excommunication in 1545 and 1543. On Luther's views regarding consecration in general, see Jürgen Diestelmann, *Actio Sacramentalis: Die Verwaltung des Heiligen Abendmahles nach den Prinzipien Martin Luthers in der Zeit bis zur Konkordienformel* (Gross Oesingen: Lutherische Buchhandlung H. Harms, 1996).

Testament—the ordained ministry is a public service of word and sacraments within and over against God's people. Generally, the *rite vocatus* principle of AC Article XIV is one of the most neglected parts of the Reformation heritage. This principle clearly excludes the practice, in some churches quite widespread, of lay presidency at the Eucharist.

In concluding, I would like to repeat my allegation that hardly any theological issue has been exposed to such a massive shift in comparison with the original message of the Reformers as ecclesiology. This is due partly to the unavoidable ecclesiological implications of a radically personalized theology, but also to a proclivity among Protestants to base their understanding of the Church more or less exclusively on the one-sidedly critical statements of Martin Luther—such as his indication that "church" is a "blind word"—while neglecting his affirmations of the Church's key role in the mediation of salvation. Moreover, the Augsburg Confession, let alone its Apology, hardly plays any role at all in Protestant deliberations. Clearly occasional and contextual utterances by Luther are falsely presented as if they were elements of a complete theological ecclesiology. Generally, the liberal-pietistic straitjacket of contemporary Protestantism has led to a massive ecclesiological vacuum. This vacuum has had far-reaching consequences in regard to the Protestant project as a whole. While the presence of a sacramental foundation and an ecclesial framework somehow manages to keep things together in the lives of the churches, the absence of such a framework tends to lead to things falling apart at maximum speed. As I see it, this is one of the main features of today's liberal-pietism, and it offers little hope for the future.

Cultural Pragmatism, Iconoclasm, and the Nature of Protestantism

Some may see the following section as a digression from the central concern of this book. And I admit that the following questions—crucial, I think—will be dealt with in a far too cursory manner. However, I would like to stress that what is at stake at this point is most relevant to my emphasis on the Church's basic visibility and the consequent almost "empirical" nature of our life in Christ. The key concern is the role of culture and cultural expression in manifesting and mediating this visibility. And I would argue that the Protestant position in this respect, one consistent with its insistence that the Church should be understood largely as an invisible and therefore abstract entity, is an additional sign of its inability to account for the present concern.

A feasible staring point in this regard is the aesthetic—and theological—principle that was laid down by Michelangelo: The heart is slow to love what the eye does not see. This suggests that our ability really to cherish things still invisible to us presupposes some kind of imagery. In keeping with the decisions of the undivided church on the significance and use of icons, it becomes clear that such images do not violate the first commandment. One may suggest that one of the key tasks of the Church is to contribute to, and provide the required space for, such imagery. Seen in this perspective, cultural expression emerges as more than practical means. Cultural expression should rather be perceived as a factor that contributes to the essential visibility of the Church.

Now, in dealing with the cultural implications of the Reformation, the most sensible place to start is music. However, even in this respect the cultural ambiguity of the Reformation movement comes to the fore. On the one hand, there can be little doubt that music played a crucial role in the Lutheran Reformation and that Martin Luther himself was genuinely fond of music. This is confirmed by the works of composers like Bach, Schütz, and Praetorius, as well as by numerous statements by Luther on the significance of music and his own musical offerings. On the other hand, there is much evidence that this positive assessment does not concern music per se, but rather its potential *function* in serving what to Luther was vastly more important, namely, the word or the preaching of the gospel. Accordingly, it may be argued that music was largely conceived as a "crutch" or even as a "bait" for God's word, reducing it to the level of pure *means*.[13] Let me at this point add that the famous Austrian conductor Nikolaus Harnoncourt has argued that Johann Sebastian Bach should be understood just as much as a product of what may be labeled a southern German Catholic "mass culture" as a "fruit of the Reformation."

A similar ambiguity can be traced in the Lutheran attitude toward images and visual arts. On the one hand, few of the Lutheran Reformers participated directly in the iconoclasm or *Bildersturm* of the Radical Reformation. And even if artists like Cranach the Elder, Dürer, and Furttnagel, in their portraits of the Reformers, clearly aimed at contributing to a kind of Reformation iconography, several of their works, such as Dürer's woodcut illustrations of the Apocalypse, were of significantly innovative religious importance. On the other hand, it can be

---

[13] Such or similar expressions have been used by the Norwegian musicologist Finn Benestad in *Musikk og tanke* (Oslo: Aschehoug, 1979).

argued that parts of Martin Luther's theology at least implicitly served as a kind of ideological foundation and source of inspiration for the iconoclasts. And this largely depended on the fact that Luther also in this field argued for a functional approach that implied that the artistic and religious value of works that did not correspond with his theological convictions tended to be overruled, occasionally even rejecting images and accepting their destruction.[14] When the proposed "pragmatic functionalism" was taken over and adapted by the Radical Reformers, iconoclasm emerged as a natural consequence. This is, among other things, reflected in the immense fury of the iconoclasts against images of the Holy Virgin and the saints that is excessively documented in the vast number of decapitated statues in European churches.[15]

Regardless of certain exceptions, Luther's cultural pragmatic functionalism was adopted and in many ways radicalized by Protestants and liberal-pietists, emerging parallel to their adherence to Puritan "God-fearing modesty" and other elements of what Max Weber saw as the core of a Protestant ethics. This is also reflected in the gospel-based pragmatism, the sterile minimalism, and the inclination toward abstraction that mark Protestantism. As the Christian life is embedded "within" us, visibility plays a clearly modest role in Protestant theology and piety. Today this position has been combined with massively populist currents as well as a kind of cultural nostalgia. This has left us with a Christian culture in which the aim is either popular acclaim and communicability that pays little attention to the basic criteria of cultural value, or with a predominantly nostalgic approach that consists of an unrestricted appetite for Gregorian chant and an admiration for composers with a boundless love of the past, such as Arvo Pärt and John

---

[14] This is even reflected in Luther's 1525 attack on Karlstadt and the Radical Reformation in *Against the Heavenly Prophets in the Matter of Images and Sacraments,* where, among other things, he affirms that he would not object to the destruction of images as long as this could be done orderly and without too much fuss—*Luther's Works* 41 (Philadelphia: Fortress Press, 1958). Later on, especially after his visitations in Saxony in 1527–1529, radical excesses may have provoked a certain shift in Luther's view. This, however, did not lead to an explicitly positive theology of images, but at most to a return to the "pragmatic functionalism" that, in my opinion, characterizes the Reformers' cultural attitude in general.

[15] This fury and the ambivalence of the Lutheran Reformers toward images and its impact on the iconoclasts were forcefully documented in an exhibition on *Bildersturm* in Bern and Strasbourg in 2000–2001. See the comprehensive and most valuable catalogue from the exhibition, *Bildersturm—Wahnsinn oder Gottes Wille? Katalog zur Ausstellung, Bernisches Historisches Museum und Museum de l'Oevre Notre Dame* (Bern, 2000).

Tavener. This takes place at the cost of renewing impulses from musicians like James MacMillan, Petr Eben, and Sofia Gubaidulina.

Ironically, however, the resulting impoverishment of cultural life in churches and congregations may easily prove to have negative repercussions for the gospel simply because there is a limit to how often the Christian message can be fused with Gounod's *Ave Maria* or Albinoni's *Adagio* without losing its power. Moreover, cultural expressions cannot be seen as solely saccharine illustrations of the gospel. Such expressions must rather have the capacity to bring the *real* world into the Church and its worship. A so-called "modernist" culture, as found, for example, within early twentieth-century German Expressionism and its proxies, may prove to be of particular significance, since this culture, according to Theodor Adorno, reflects the sufferings of today's human beings in a special manner. There is a strong need for renewal within Protestant cultural life. Without such a renewal, the possibility for churches to stand forth as salt and light in the world will be notably reduced.

These brief deliberations on culture can well be summarized by quoting the British Roman Catholic and somewhat eccentric artist Eric Gill, who has achieved fame for his Stations of the Cross in London's Westminster Cathedral:

> I became a Catholic because I fell in love with the truth. And love is an experience. I saw. I heard. I felt. I tasted. I touched. And that is what lovers do. Lest anyone should think that in this devotion to the Mass, to the Blessed Sacrament, to the Holy Eucharist I am devoted to an abstraction, to a purely intellectual and even aesthetic Catholicism (not that such things are to be despised or rejected) I must say this: the Real Presence which we affirm is the real presence of the man Jesus. Let no one suppose that because we adore him in the spirit we do not adore him in our hearts. Very God, yes. And dear Jesus also. He speaks to us and we speak to him. We kiss the hem of his garment, we also thank him for our bread and butter. He ordained that our bodily motions should be pleasant and gratifying. He ordained the thunderstorms and the lion's voracity; he also blessed the daisies and the poor. He sits in judgement; he is also friend and brother.[16]

I shall resist the temptation to argue that this statement shows that Roman Catholicism today represents a far more open and constructive

---

[16] *Eric Gill: An Autobiography* (New York: Devin-Adair Company, 1941) 247.

cultural attitude than Protestantism. The key concern here is that Gill shows how crucial the empirical nature of the Christian life and the corresponding visibility of the Church is, not least theologically. And as this essential visibility is mediated *inter alia* through art and culture, there is a need to move beyond the cultural pragmatism of the Reformation in its present Protestant disguise.

Renewal Movement without Renewal Potential?

Admittedly, my assessment so far has not only been presented in a brief and almost categorical way, it has also been marked by certain limitations. The most obvious one is that I have dealt primarily with the situation in the Lutheran churches in Europe and North America. On the one hand, it can be argued that the situation is better elsewhere, perhaps particularly among African Lutherans. Yet, impulses from these churches seem to have played a fairly modest role in Europe and North America. Furthermore, I realize that Protestantism and Lutheranism cannot be flatly identified, yet as I have tried to show, there is much evidence that a massive "Protestantization" has taken place among Lutherans especially in the late nineteenth and early twentieth centuries, and especially in the form of the influential liberal-pietistic alliance. This current still plays a leading role in our churches, while what may be labeled as "high church" or "evangelical-catholic" positions have been radically marginalized almost everywhere in the Lutheran world in an astonishingly short time.

As a conclusion, I would like to present for further reflection and discussion the following observations and theses concerning the prospects of the Reformation. (1) The difference between authentic Reformation theology and what today is labeled "Lutheran" is often so huge that there is much evidence that we face a totally *new* movement. (2) Regardless of how correct it may be, an insistence on the catholicity and ecumenicity of the Reformation at present appears to be primarily of academic interest, simply because this position has become increasingly marginal and invisible in the concrete lives of the Lutheran churches. (3) Today many of the central concerns of the Reformers seem to be implemented more effectively outside rather than within the Reformation churches. In my view, this is particularly the case within the Roman Catholic Church as presented through the Second Vatican Council. (4) As already indicated, the raison d'être as well as the future of the Reformation is closely connected with its actual potential for renewal. However, both the Lutheran churches and the Lutheran communion at large seem increasingly to have lost such potential. (5) This indicates that the Reformation project may be approaching its end. The Reformation churches can, of course, continue to exist on the basis of their present platform, but for those who defend a catholic interpretation of the Reformation, other ways must probably be sought.

It is hard to say whether the development of the Reformation movement is the result of an integral discrepancy or the result of a process of decay. In any case, the rather gloomy picture presented above is a source of considerable sadness. But this is how I see things. And it would not serve any constructive purpose just to sweep these observations under the carpet. For a long time I held ecumenical contacts and impulses to be a possible way of rescuing and safeguarding the true catholicity and ecumenicity of the Reformation. However, I must confess that I have more or less lost that hope. We are frequently confronted with evidence which indicates that what can be harvested ecumenically has already been harvested; there seems to be little more to gain. After a quite promising period in the 1990s, more recent years have been marked by notable setbacks within Lutheran ecumenism, a point to be developed further in Chapter 4 below. The most important challenge now is to try to indicate a new approach forward for ecumenically committed evangelical catholic Lutherans. This crucial concern will be addressed in the next chapter of this book.

Chapter 2

"The Great Tradition of the Church"
An Old Way Forward?

The previous chapter presented a picture of a substantial crisis within the contemporary Reformation movement, particularly in its Protestant shape. What is being referred to as "Lutheran" today often appears to be at such a distance from the catholicity and ecumenicity of the Reformers that it emerges in effect as a new movement. And the influential current of "liberal-pietism" offers a striking picture of what happens when positions that lack ecclesial and sacramental anchors start to disintegrate: disintegration takes place at an incredible speed. As a result of such developments, many feel more and more homeless in their own churches, not only theologically but also in terms of worship life.

Accordingly, we have to look for alternative ways to maintain the Reformers' vision both of a renewal movement within the one church and of a consistent worshiping fellowship. Such alternatives must be grounded in the faith of the Church that has been expressed through the ages, and they must also be able to present that faith in ways that make sense today. There must also be an ecumenical openness combined with a firm commitment to the truth. And there must be an ecclesial and sacramental basis that offers sustainable forms of piety and spiritual life.

In this connection, it is worthwhile to consider what has been labeled "the Great Tradition of the Church." Theologically, this position has much in common with the movement known as "evangelical catholicity" that emerged particularly during the first half of the twentieth century. Structurally, however, and in terms of basic aims, this position cannot be seen as identical with the Reformation movement. Its orientation is clearly ecumenical, not necessarily breaking with the Lutheran tradition but going significantly beyond it. What is important to the Great Tradition is not primarily to rescue authentic Reformation theology, but rather to place viable parts of its heritage in a wider and richer framework.

In the following I shall convey an interpretation of the Great Tradition of the Church and its parallel, evangelical catholicity, focusing mainly on the theological content and structural implications of these currents. At the outset it is important to stress that the option of the Great Tradition should not be understood merely as a possible basis of a practical church-political alliance between conservative Evangelicals, traditionalist Anglicans, and high church Lutherans. Rather, the possibility is open that within these frames a comprehensive ecumenical program and a new ecclesial platform can be established that transcend traditional denominational borders. It remains to be seen, however, where this will lead in terms of church membership.

Evangelical Catholicity—Still a Valid Option?

It is difficult to trace the roots of the term "evangelical catholicity," simply because many of those who have been associated with this term hardly ever used it.[1] This can be demonstrated in regard to the so-called neo-Lutheranism or the conservative "high orthodoxy" of the latter part of the nineteenth century. The leading neo-Lutheran theologian Friedrich Julius Stahl even applied the term in question to describe the opposite of what he saw as authentic or "real" Catholicism. However, when it came to theology and especially to the interpretation of the Reformation, high orthodoxy was crucial to the development of evangelical catholicity. This was also the case with regard to Wilhelm Löhe and later figures like Hans Asmussen, Wilhelm Stählin, and Ernst Kinder. In the United States, both Paul Tillich and Jaroslav Pelikan have focused on the dialectic between "protestant principle" and "catholic substance." Evangelical catholicity has often been used to describe what was held to be an authentic interpretation of the Lutheran Reformation and of

---

[1] Obviously, we cannot go into the concept of evangelical catholicity in detail here. The following account is partly based on Sven-Erik Brodd, *Evangelisk Katolicitet. Ett studium av innehåll och funktion under 1800-och 1900-talen* (Uppsala: CWK Gleerup, 1982). See also Carl E. Braaten, "Die Katholizität der Reformation: Der Ort der Reformation in der Bewegung der Evangelischen Katholiken," *Kerygma und Dogma* 42 (1996) 186ff.

the Augsburg Confession in particular. It assumed a critical distance not only from Protestantism but also from Roman Catholicism, and it often revealed limited concern for the fathers and theology of the ancient church. Thus, one may argue, the term "evangelical catholicity" was close to being coopted by confessionalistic Lutherans.

There are, however, examples of an ecumenically far more open application of the concept, for example, in the discussions concerning the Nicene Creed's third mark of the Church, catholicity, which took place early within the Faith and Order Movement. Also, the program for a reunited church envisaged by the Swedish archbishop Nathan Söderblom (1866–1931) identified the three mainstreams of Christianity as Greek Catholic, Roman Catholic, and Evangelical Catholic. The notion of evangelical catholicity played a central role within Swedish Lutheranism throughout the twentieth century.[2] Here the Swedish Förbundet för Kristen Enhet-Gemenskap (the Association for Christian Unity-Fellowship), with its plan for reunification with the Roman Catholic Church, represents a most challenging approach.[3] The ecumenical potential of evangelical catholicity is further reflected in its similarities with the nineteenth-century Oxford Movement and subsequent

[2] In addition to theologians and church leaders like Yngve Brilioth, Hjalmar Lindroth, Anders Nygren, Gustaf Aulén, and Bo Giertz, all associated with *den nya kyrkosynen* ("the new understanding of the church") which emerged during the middle of the twentieth century within the Church of Sweden and which at least partly had its roots in the so-called *ungkyrko-rörelsen* ("the young church movement"), Gunnar Rosendal, in my opinion, calls for particular attention here. Regrettably, however, Rosendal's work is not available in English.

[3] This association or movement (FKE-G) was formed in 1972 and was established theologically in the Swedish high church tradition with its vision of evangelical catholicity. It developed, however, into a program that sought union with the Roman Catholic Church; some have described this program as a kind of collective scheme for conversion that included more than thirty ordained priests of the Church of Sweden. At the core of this scheme was a wish to seek reunion with the Catholic Church and the Bishop of Rome, while keeping parts of the Lutheran and Swedish heritage. During the process, a comprehensive ecumenical model was developed that aimed at the accomplishment of these goals. A statement with the title "Katolsk tro i Svenska kyrkan" ("Catholic Faith in the Church of Sweden") was published in 1973. The whole initiative had a certain resemblance to the German Bund für evangelisch-katholische Wiedervereinigung (Association for Evangelical-Catholic Reunion), led by Max Lackmann. However, after extensive talks with representatives of the Vatican, the conclusion was that the scheme could not be realized. Some of the participants converted individually, others aimed at building catholic communities within the Church of Sweden, and some returned to their service in this church. An account and evaluation of this challenging process can be found in Nils-Henrik Lindblad, *En svensk ekumenisk model* (Uppsala: The Nordic Ecumenical Institute, 1984).

Anglo-Catholicism, and partly also with the "Liberal Catholicism" of Charles Gore. Moreover, the term "Northern Catholicism," used as a designation for all non-Roman, Western European high church movements, can in certain respects be seen as an implicit attempt to broaden the scope at this point.[4] Still, it is hard to overlook the distance from Rome that marks at least some versions of evangelical catholicity.

The person who more than anyone else contributed to filling the concept of evangelical catholicity with substance was the German theologian and church leader Friedrich Heiler (1882–1967).[5] His background was truly ecumenical. He grew up in a Roman Catholic home, became an evangelical Lutheran by conversion, and had a keen interest in Orthodox spirituality. Heiler's conversion was partly motivated by impulses from his teacher and friend Nathan Söderblom and from the Swedish high church movement, but also by an increasingly critical attitude toward what he experienced as stern Roman Catholic institutionalism. Although he had refused professorships in systematic theology at Evangelical faculties in Germany because that might jeopardize his wish to stand "between the churches," Rudolf Otto convinced him to accept a chair in the history and philosophy of religion departments in Marburg. His studies in this field led to a strong concern for Christian mysticism and its corresponding spirituality. However, most important was Heiler's long period of leadership in the Hochkirchliche Vereinigung (the German High Church Association) and his involvement in the ecumenical movement. It should also be noted that Friedrich Heiler was one of the church leaders who protested most strongly against the Nazi government before and during the Second World War, a reflection of the sound social commitment of several high church groups.[6]

---

[4] See N. P. Williams and Charles Harris, eds., *Northern Catholicism: Centenary Studies in the Oxford Movement and Parallel Movements* (London: SPCK, 1933). In addition to several contributions dealing with the Oxford Movement of the nineteenth century, this important book contains essays on the "German catholic movement" by Friedrich Heiler, Reformed high church currents in Holland and Scotland, Methodism, and the Old Catholic Church, but, rather conspicuously, not on the most "Northern" form of Catholicism, that is, Swedish evangelical catholicity.

[5] On Heiler see Hans Hartog, *Evangelische Katholizität. Weg und Vision Friedrich Heilers* (Mainz: Grünewald, 1995). Among Heiler's works, the following call for particular attention: *Das Wesen des Katholizismus* (1920), *Katholischer und Evangelischer Gottesdienst* (1921), and *Evangelische Katholizität* (1926).

[6] This was particularly the case with regard to the Oxford Movement. Generally, the social commitment in question functions as a correction of the quite common picture of the high church groups as being marked by a rather narrow ecclesial concern and scope. Moreover, it clearly contributes to the visibility of this movement.

Theologically, Heiler saw evangelical catholicity as an intermediate position between Roman Catholic institutionalism and Protestant minimalism. He criticized the Roman Catholic Church for being syncretistic, since it included both "primitive ritualism" and "Judaic legalism." At the same time, he accused Martin Luther of isolating the gospel from "Catholic fullness" by placing it on "a throne of solitude." According to Heiler, "evangelical" was virtually identical with the *sola gratia* principle, while "Catholic" served as an expression of the Church's fullness. He saw that in the Augsburg Confession especially these two concerns were held together in a most fruitful way. His aim was to develop a kind of synthesis, a church with "evangelical soul and catholic body," or in another formulation, a catholic church that was "cleansed" by an evangelical spirit. Seen in an ecumenical perspective, Heiler's vision comes through as largely federative along the lines of the so-called branch theory, in which the different churches were perceived as incorporating specific values that contribute to the fullness of the Church. This federative vision was also marked by efforts to realize intercommunion between the churches.

Heiler's vision, however, did not consist solely of theological ideas. For him, evangelical catholicity also included a particular spirituality and a sacramentally grounded piety, as well as a concrete ecclesiological program. In due course, these concerns were structurally embodied in the High Church Association and the newly founded Evangelish-Katholische Eucharistische Gemeinschaft (the Evangelical Catholic Eucharistic Fellowship). There was strong emphasis on the episcopal office in general and on the need to contribute to a restoration of the historic succession in particular. After some hesitation Heiler was himself ordained in 1930 as a bishop or a spiritual episcopal visitor for the Evangelical Catholic movement, with bishops who stood in historic succession participating in the ceremony. Internally this event was considered a vital contribution in securing appropriate pastoral oversight; externally it was seen to be an important ecumenical sign. As underscored in Hans Hartog's biography of Heiler, a central point was to show that Heiler and his followers were prepared to act, not only to talk, despite harshly negative reactions by some who held the consecration to be divisive.[7]

The next year, the sacramental spirituality that Heiler advocated found concrete expression in a new order for the celebration of the

---

[7] See Hartog, *Evangelische Katholizität*, 41: "bei uns wird nicht mehr nur geredet, sondern gehandelt."

Holy Mass in the Evangelical Catholic Eucharistic Fellowship. This liturgical order was designed to make certain that members of the Fellowship could celebrate the Eucharist in a way corresponding to their faith, a possibility largely denied to them in the German Lutheran churches. The Evangelical Catholic movement established its own forms for episcopal oversight and eucharistic celebration even as it insisted on remaining within the Lutheran Church as a movement for catholic and ecumenical renewal.

Obviously, Friedrich Heiler was a child of his time, inasmuch as his theology included unmistakably idealistic elements. I am convinced, however, that he still has much to contribute, partly in regard to certain aspects of his interpretation of the Reformation, but mainly in regard to his ecclesiological and ecumenical vision of renewal. Against this background, it is sad to note that only about thirty-five years after Heiler's death the movement he founded was radically marginalized within his own German church. Actually, this seems also to have been the case with expressions of the evangelical catholic movement in most Lutheran churches, with Sweden and certain initiatives in the United States, notably the Center for Catholic and Evangelical Theology, as the main exceptions.

This shift has been substantial and rapid. While evangelical catholic impulses played quite a central role a few decades ago in the work of theologians like Edmund Schlink, Regin Prenter, and Arthur Carl Piepkorn, such impulses have almost no influence today. Why is this so? Obviously, there are several reasons. A most central one may well be that a crucial lesson from Friedrich Heiler and his movement has been forgotten: renewal cannot come about solely by reflecting and talking; authentic renewal can only be achieved by doing and acting. This, moreover, requires some sort of concrete structural embodiment, even to the point of establishing alternative forms of pastoral-episcopal oversight and sustaining a spiritual life through special orders for eucharistic celebration.

Admittedly, the serious catch with such initiatives is that they may become church dividing. This, however, should not be seen as an unavoidable consequence, except in those cases where the required foundation of community in shared faith, common sacramental life, and joint mission has been lost beyond rescue and unity only survives within a practical-administrative framework. Moreover, if we are serious about the catholic vision of renewal that derives from the Reformation heritage, there may be few other options in today's situation than the establishment of viable alternatives to the status quo. It is precisely for this reason that the Great Tradition of the Church calls for particular attention, since it may well emerge as perhaps the best way of realizing today what the evangelical catholic movement was aiming at fifty years ago.

The Great Tradition of the Church—Theological Content

The term "the Great Tradition of the Church" has occasionally been used in theological discourse and debate, particularly in the United States.[8] However, the term is not unambiguously clear. As already indicated, it quite often comes across primarily as a largely practical effort to identify a strategic basis for cooperation between conservative Evangelicals and various high church groups or as a somewhat defensive attempt to rescue the remnants of classical Christianity. In the following reflections I will attempt to widen this scope in an ecclesial and ecumenical direction. The Great Tradition of the Church should first be seen as an identification of what may develop into a new ecclesiological platform with an integral spirituality. Second, it includes an ecumenical program that takes us beyond the traditional borders between churches or denominations. Third, it can at least implicitly be regarded as an effort to reinterpret and revitalize the vision of evangelical catholicity.

In an attempt to contribute to a more precise definition of the Great Tradition, the following reflections, it is hoped, will prove helpful as regards the theological content as well as the structural implications of the concept. However, it is important to underline that the present account should be seen as no more than a preliminary proposal or sketch. There is an obvious need for other approaches and contributions, not least since we are dealing with a concept that aims to reflect the vast richness of the Church's faith and witness across time and space and also to offer a comprehensive ecumenical program. Our presentation takes the form of ten brief theses.

1) The Great Tradition of the Church is grounded in the apostolic witness to Christ as ultimately revealed in Holy Scripture and living

---

[8] An example of this can be found in James S. Cutsinger, ed., *Reclaiming the Great Tradition: Evangelicals, Catholics and Orthodox in Dialogue* (Downers Grove, Ill.: InterVarsity Press, 1997). See also the journal *Touchstone: A Journal of Mere Christianity.* Obviously, "the Great Tradition" draws primarily from what was first termed, at the World Conference on Faith and Order held in Montreal in 1963, as "Tradition with capital T," without in any sense ignoring the traditions of the different churches.

on in the Church's *anamnesis*—its memorial—expressed in liturgy, tradition, and witness. There is a dialectic between Scripture as foundation and the Church's witness to that foundation.

2) The Great Tradition of the Church is defined and shaped by the ecumenical creeds of the ancient and undivided church, mainly the *Nicenum,* but also the *Apostolicum* and the *Athanasianum,* which express the fundamental trinitarian and christological witness of the ancient church as a whole. Accordingly, later denominational confessional writings must be seen primarily as contextualized implementations of the ecumenical creeds. This also means that what has been labeled, in the Faith and Order Movement, as Tradition with a capital "T" is prior to the traditions, with a small "t," of the churches.

3) The Great Tradition of the Church is fundamentally catholic in the sense that it aims at incorporating the faith of the church in all its richness across time as well as space. It therefore transcends all reductionist or minimalist positions. It sees Christ as the living center that helps us to maintain, understand, and rejoice in the Church's deposit of faith, correcting a narrow christomonistic approach that effectively cuts us off from this rich treasure.

4) The Great Tradition of the Church is sacramentally, ecclesiologically, and liturgically based, which means that it insists that participation in the fruits of Christ's sacrifice takes place through word and sacrament in the space of the church. This is in accordance with St. Cyprian's vital observation: "You cannot have God for your father unless you have the church for your mother" (*On the Unity of the Church,* 6). It also corresponds to St. Augustine's crucial dictum: *Qui cantat bis orat* (*Explanations of the Psalms* 72, 1)—the one who sings, as part of the church's liturgy, prays twice as strongly.

5) The Great Tradition of the Church realizes that the people of God are a structured people in the sense that pastoral leaders and shepherds as well as laity are included. The priestly character and service of all the faithful are affirmed along with the essential need for an effective spiritual leadership exercised with authority and love through the ordained ministries that God has instituted. These ministries are located in the midst of God's people and for their benefit. However, the Great Tradition is careful not to destroy the subtle balance between these two types of ministry by confusing them.

6) The Great Tradition of the Church is based on the firm conviction that the Church, in accordance with its nature, is one, and it acknowledges a fundamental ecumenical obligation. It is clearly aware

of the fact that heresy jeopardizes the Church and its identity, consequently constituting the ultimate borderline of community in Christ.

7) The Great Tradition of the Church holds God's will to be binding and obligatory for human life in its totality. And it acknowledges its commission to preach God's law, which is to affirm its responsibility to confront all violations of the goodwill of God the Creator with his call to repentant lives renewed to his glory and the benefit of all humankind.

8) The Great Tradition of the Church places significant weight on the Church's sending, mission, and service in the world. In light of this, the Church is summoned and equipped to stand forth as the priest of creation, as the first fruit of a reunited humankind, and as *sacramentum mundi,* a sacrament or a sacramental sign in and for the world. Strong social commitment is a hallmark of the Great Tradition.

9) The Great Tradition of the Church realizes that the dialectic between creation and redemption provides the framework of the Church's mission. The aim of this mission is not only that a number of souls be saved, but that God's creation will be redeemed. The Church must make room for and provide a voice for the world's longing for redemption.

10) The Great Tradition of the Church should never be perceived as a purely nostalgic project. Being firmly fixed in the witness and shape of the ancient church, it also looks both outward to the people and the world it is called to serve, and forward to the time of eschatological fulfillment, when Christ returns in order to bring his work to completion.

It is along lines like these that the theological substance of the Great Tradition of the Church must be defined. This concept may occasionally move somewhat beyond the theology of the Lutheran Reformation, but it does not imply a radical break with that tradition. It is clearly in keeping with the vision of renewal found in evangelical catholicity, although it has a wider ecumenical scope than some interpretations of that vision. Moreover, it corresponds to the theology of several churches and groups that adhere to catholic and orthodox faith. It must clearly be pointed out, however, that the Great Tradition of the Church is not necessarily "great" in the sense that all or even most contemporary churches and Christians immediately will feel at home in it. It is "great" in the sense that it includes the key elements of what may be labeled "classic Christianity," aiming to present those elements in a form that makes sense today. In the view of this author, the

Great Tradition of the Church represents by far the most appropriate way of uncovering the vast richness of the Church's treasure of faith.

The Great Tradition of the Church—Structural Implications

Admittedly, it is more difficult to describe possible structural implications of the Great Tradition of the Church than to say something about its content. However, it has already been underlined that what is at stake here are not only abstract theological ideas. This means that commitment to the Great Tradition must and will have structural implications on more than one level: regarding the identification and evaluation of appropriate church structures in general and also regarding the structural visibility of a renewal movement begun in this "Tradition." The key concern is the strong obligation of the Great Tradition to the essential visibility of the Church in general and the goal of visible unity in particular. Again, this can be specified by some theses, or rather by examples of feasible structural consequences.

1) Stemming from its emphasis on ecclesial visibility, the Great Tradition of the Church is fully committed to the goal of visible unity. It realizes that both this visible unity and the Church's visibility as such are structurally manifested, although visibility is not to be completely identified with structures. There are, to be sure, structures that only serve the maintenance and perpetuation of denominational or parochial church institutions. The obligation to visible unity, however, implies that such parochially conditioned structures are definitely secondary to structures of unity. Accordingly, a distinction between different structural levels is needed.[9] This does not necessarily mean that the so-called Christian World Communions, for example, the Anglican Consultative Council and the Lutheran World Federation, become illegitimate, even if such bodies can never be seen as isolated ends in themselves. However, these and other bodies must always be directed toward a greater goal: the visible structured unity of all God's children.

2) The Great Tradition of the Church emphasizes the office of the bishop as a key bond of unity and continuity in the Church's life. This aspect of unity is connected with the bishop's service in representing the local church universally and the universal Church locally. Here the model of the early church of "one bishop in each place" plays a crucial

---

[9] On the suggested structural differentiation, see, among others, Edmund Schlink, *Ökumenische Dogmatik: Grundzüge* (Göttingen: Vandenhoeck & Ruprecht, 1983) 558ff.

role. Yet in light of the later development in the divided church of parallel episcopal jurisdictions, it must be asked whether or not the unity of the local episcopate can also be maintained and safeguarded within a collegial framework. The aspect of continuity expressed through the historic episcopate is a sign of the apostolic succession of the whole church.

3) According to the New Testament, the Church is essentially both local and universal. While the bishop, as we have seen, serves mainly the local unity, though always with a view to a wider universal perspective, there is also need for a special universal service to or ministry of unity. The Great Tradition of the Church is, therefore, open to the possibility that visible community on the universal level requires some kind of unity with the Bishop of Rome, the successor of Peter. This should not be perceived as a unity *under* Rome, but as a unity *with* Rome, in which "the Western patriarch" has a special responsibility for the Church's universal unity within the framework of a comprehensive collegial and synodal structure.

4) Since the Great Tradition of the Church strongly stresses the Church's mission and service in the world, there is a legitimate inclination toward a certain structural flexibility that presupposes a dynamic approach so that the need for stability is always balanced with a concern for mobility. All ecclesial structures are supposed to facilitate and not hamper the Church's mission.

5) It has repeatedly been pointed out that commitment to the Great Tradition of the Church may and will take us significantly beyond traditional church borders. Accordingly, this commitment opens up many new constellations. Ecumenical implications of this development will be discussed in more detail in the next section of this chapter. However, already at this stage it is important to note strongly that those who belong together in terms of faith and spirituality must also be allowed to be together without prejudice or artificial barriers.

Ultimately, most of these structural implications can be fully realized only within a proper church or within the framework of visible ecclesial communion. We have noted that Friedrich Heiler's evangelical catholic vision included intermediate structural provisions, for example, concrete forms of pastoral-episcopal oversight and a distinct liturgical order for the celebration of the Eucharist. The fact that such structural initiatives can lead to division presents an immense challenge that may eventually force choices between relative evils. The key concern here, however, is simply that a movement around an ecumenically based proposal for visible church unity must itself possess basic visibility. And this means that the requirement for structural manifestations cannot be ignored.

The Great Tradition of the Church—Ecumenical Potential

It has already been indicated that the Great Tradition of the Church has both positive and problematic implications when seen in ecumenical perspective. The key asset of this concept is that it takes us beyond traditional denominational borderlines, having the capacity to unite faithful from several traditions who in faith and spiritual life clearly belong together. Moreover, it expresses and safeguards the diachronic unity of the Church across time. In this sense, the present approach is capable of serving the wider ecumenical movement in a highly positive way.

Simultaneously, the commitment of the Great Tradition to offer an option for renewal that may include a specific ecclesial platform and a distinct spiritual life, together with a firm resolution to make this option concretely and structurally visible, can lead, and in many cases has already led, to internal tensions and even division within churches. This is clearly a regrettable outcome. Yet it would be meaningless to claim that such tensions are created by, or have their origin in, the Great Tradition of the Church as such; this would be tantamount to arguing that the Church's deposit of faith is itself divisive. Obviously, new lines of division and new forms of fellowship that transcend traditional church borders are increasingly important today. When some insist that adherence to the Great Tradition is divisive, it should be pointed out that division is also often the result of the widespread preference for the highly influential liberal-pietistic alliance, an alliance that is in massive discontinuity with the faith of the Church through the ages.

There is a significant amount of irony or even tragedy to an ecumenically directed renewal movement that may result in division. However, this is nothing new in the Church's life, particularly when one is concerned to hold ecumenical commitment firmly together with obligation to the truth. In light of the inherent and unavoidable schismatic implications of heresy, we must always be prepared to face such consequences. Moreover, the experience of the Great Tradition as divisive also reflects that this current has been massively marginalized in several churches almost to the point of excommunication, especially on the European continent and also somewhat in North America. This is often a result of efforts to compensate for doctrinal confusion by insisting on uniformity in order. On the Protestant side there is a tendency to cherish diversity externally in order to provide space for one's own identity, while being far more restrictive with respect to internal "catholic" initiatives. In light of this, it should be noted that on the one hand the Great Tradition of the Church possesses an obvious formal similarity to the intention of the Lutheran Reformation, while on the other hand it deviates radically from a so-called postmodern, Protestant adoration of "pluralism" and its subsequent sensitivity to political correctness.

In the present situation there is perhaps no other option than to appeal to generosity and plain human decency. Within the mainline churches, an example of this can be found in the appointment of so-called "flying bishops" within the Church of England to provide episcopal oversight for those who oppose the ordination of women. This is clearly not a perfect theological solution, but it reflects a genuine concern for generosity that should definitely not be seen as foreign or irrelevant to the Church. In the Church of Norway, however, such a solution was regrettably turned down, leading to a significant number of withdrawals from the Church and even to the formation of a new church. I am not familiar with any Lutheran church that has been willing to provide alternative forms of episcopal oversight, often forcing renewal groups to establish structures of their own.

Similarly, among adherents of the Great Tradition a certain inclination toward retrenchment or even sectarianism can be detected, an inclination that in some cases has been combined with rather aggressive, almost militant attitudes. Such attitudes often emerge as signs of massive disappointment and desperation, but they nevertheless clearly contradict the nature as well as the aim of the Great Tradition. There may be a need for a reminder that patience and humility are true Christian virtues. The ecumenical relevance of the unifying gifts of the Spirit as they are listed in Galatians 5:22ff., in opposition to the divisive "desires of self-indulgence," is of crucial significance here.

Is it possible, then, to say anything definite regarding the implications of the Great Tradition for church membership? Attempts to offer clear answers depend on a number of external and quite uncertain factors, such as the attitudes of churches in which renewal movements anchored in the Great Tradition have been established, the response especially of the Roman Catholic Church and the Orthodox Churches to these groups, and general ecumenical developments. In light of the history and present practice of catholic renewal movements, three options emerge: (1) One may choose to remain in the church one belongs to provided that a certain space is made for the renewal vision that is at stake. (2) One may seek fellowship and build cross-structures with the faithful in other churches who share one's faith and spirituality. Some will reject this option as an effort to establish a new denomination, but this may be countered by the genuine ecumenical character of the Great Tradition of the Church and the plain fact that this concept is no new invention. (3) The whole venture may lead to individual or collective conversions—in some cases even to the formation of new churches—if the necessary space for the proposed vision is denied. Obviously, this must be seen as an emergency solution, but it can also be understood as an expression of a theological realism that simply accepts the fact that in the long run church fellowship cannot be maintained when basic unity in faith and spiritual life is missing.

It remains to be seen which of these options will prevail among proponents of the Great Tradition. None of them should be excluded in a situation where there is much insecurity in regard to the future of the churches. I consider the concept of the Great Tradition to be an excellent theological and ecumenical platform and the most suitable response to the current crisis of the Reformation movement. Yet I must admit to being less and less convinced that it can finally provide a workable ecclesial alternative to, or a feasible "surrogate" for, a full church life. We may eventually be forced to look elsewhere.

In concluding this section, let us once more attempt to specify the chief ecumenical assets of the Great Tradition of the Church. First, this approach corresponds with and visualizes the fact that church unity always must be perceived diachronically, as a unity across time. The Great Tradition's foundation in the theology of the early fathers and the ancient church plays a crucial role. This represents a forceful link to the churches of the Orthodox tradition and contributes effectively to filling the immense gap between the Bible and the Reformation that marks Protestantism.

Second, commitment to the Great Tradition of the Church also expresses the synchronic dimension of Christian unity as a unity that embraces the faithful in every place. This is particularly the case in view of its capacity to unite those who belong together in faith and spirituality regardless of church affiliation. It serves as a reminder that future ecumenical initiatives should not only follow traditional church borders but must also be prepared to transcend or cross them without pointing toward what might in effect be a new denomination.

Third, the theological content and sacramentally based spirituality, as well as the concrete structural implications, of the Great Tradition help in the realization of what visible church unity is: a unity that is founded on the empirically recognizable means of grace and is directed toward the world in order that it may see and believe.

The Great Tradition of the Church— Living, Organic, and Dynamic

Adherence to the Great Tradition and a corresponding evangelical catholic vision often come across as a largely retrospective concern or even as pure nostalgia. Church tradition in general and a focus on the theology of the fathers and the ancient church in particular are essential components in this connection. However, the Tradition that is at stake here cannot be understood as a more or less dead *depositum*; it should rather be construed as a dynamic and organic entity in the life of the Church. As already indicated, the Great Tradition must always be directed toward the Church's mission in the world and the ultimate eschatological fulfilment of Christ's work. Accordingly, it can also be seen as an effort to come to terms with the vital reminder of St. Bernard of Clairvaux that the Church has been equipped with eyes to look forward as well as backward.

What does the focus on the Great Tradition imply for the discussion on the relationship between Scripture and Tradition? Clearly we cannot go into this discussion in detail. I shall restrict myself to the following brief observation: On the one hand, Holy Scripture has a special and unique authority within the universe of the Church's faith. It provides the basic norm and measure for assessing and interpreting the larger Tradition, in accordance with the distinction between *norma normans* and *norma normata*. Since it possesses such an authority, Holy Scripture can also function as a critical corrective over against the Church.

On the other hand, the "Scripture alone" principle should not be understood in the perspective of "word alone" or confused with an insistence that there is the Bible and little or nothing else that contributes to the content of our faith. *Sola scriptura* must rather be seen as an effort to establish a hermeneutical center or core within the fullness of the Church's faith and witness and not as something that cuts us off from this fullness by playing Scripture off against Tradition. Throughout church history there are numerous examples that such an attitude really has led to retrospective nostalgia, for example, in the form of stern fundamentalism. Moreover, there is in today's situation much evidence that *sola scriptura* no longer is able to provide the churches and the faithful with the firm basis that the principle originally intended, simply because biblical interpretation is now characterized by an immense plurality. As a result of this—and somewhat ironically, one might add—doctrinal grounding will probably be far more accessible when Holy Scripture is approached and interpreted within the framework that is provided by the Great Tradition than if it is placed in a "word alone" vacuum or left to a multitude of conflicting interpretations.[10]

Finally, Cardinal Newman was probably right in insisting that "to be deep in history is to cease to be a Protestant."[11] This is not least attested to by the proclivity to constantly try to "reinvent the wheel" that marks contemporary Protestantism. Commitment to the Great Tradition of the Church may help rediscover the immense treasures contained in the faith of the Church through the ages. It may also help us to fill the vast historical gap that exists for Protestantism between the Bible and the time of the Reformation. Obviously, since Christian faith is a living entity and not merely an acceptance of a predefined dogmatic system, renewal and reinterpretation are required. This, however, is something other than continual reinvention that reflects a massive disregard for history. For while renewal and reinterpretation take place on a specific foundation and within a given framework, the compulsion to reinvent over and over again is not only a waste of time and resources, but it may also imply that the basic identity and continuity of the Christian faith is under threat. By remaining with the Great Tradition of the Church, this dead end can be avoided.

This account of the Great Tradition needs, obviously, to be complemented by others in regard to specific content. Moreover, unambiguous or definite answers concerning the prospects of this proposal for renewal can hardly be produced in a situation of great insecurity and instability. Yet such problems do not in any sense overrule or exclude the immense theological significance of the concept at hand, generally as well as in view of the crisis of the Reformation movement. As far as I am concerned, we here face a most appropriate continuation of

---

[10] While focusing on Scripture and church in a more general perspective, I have tried to develop some of these concerns a bit further in "Holy Scripture and the Church," *Pro Ecclesia* 10 (2001) 389ff.

[11] *An Essay on the Development of Christian Doctrine*, introduction., sect. 5.

the authentic catholicity and ecumenicity of the Reformers. In the following chapters this account of the Great Tradition of the Church will be taken further with regard to its ecclesiological foundation (Chapter 3), its ecumenical implications (Chapter 4), and its significance for spiritual life (Chapter 5).

Chapter 3

The Church—Mother of Faith
and Priest of Creation

While traditional pietists and liberals have tended to see the Church merely as a practical framework for (or sometimes even as a direct impediment to) authentic personal religiosity, there is a proclivity evident among contemporary postmodern liberal-pietists to claim that "Jesus may be okay, but the church is rather hopeless." A somewhat similar though radicalized attitude has often been adopted by those outside or at the margins of the Church. Today people often form or construct an individualized and private religiosity in which the Church plays no role. These attitudes are caused partly by an admittedly not altogether misplaced criticism of the Church's practice, but also, I believe, by a wish to keep the Christian faith at a safe distance. This can be accomplished when being a Christian is understood primarily as adherence to a constantly changing set of private beliefs or ideas. It is not so easily accomplished, however, when one gets involved in a visible, living fellowship that requires a certain degree of personal commitment. But such commitment is essential to our life in the Church.

Theologically, openness to Jesus with a simultaneous rejection of the Church clearly calls for correction. Even if Jesus and the Church are not to be flatly identified, it is utterly incorrect to separate him from the church that is his body. Moreover, life in Christ is corporate in the sense that it requires communion and a living fellowship, in accordance with the old saying *Unus Christianus nullus Christianus* ("A single Christian is no Christian"). Even the hermit saints were fully aware that they belonged to a larger community, not least in the sense that they were continually committed to praying for the Church and

39

the world. Moreover, the communal nature of Christian life and the fellowship that is offered in the Church correspond to the basic longing for community and solidarity that is a distinctive mark of human existence as ordained by God the Creator. And in a world where such fellowship has become a rare thing, the Church really has much to offer. This requires, however, that our community is made concretely visible for our fellow human beings. An invisible or abstract idea will not be of much help.

In the present chapter, our main aim is to say something about the corporate nature of Christian life, a life that is lived in *communio* with the Father through the Son and in the Spirit, a life that is implanted in our community with all the faithful across time as well as space, and a life that is lived in and for God's entire creation. Such a life cannot be lived in a vacuum. Quite the contrary, it is born, nourished, and maintained in a particular space or location, namely, the Church. This is an important reason why the Nicene Creed insists on its *credo ecclesiam.* The Church is not only an empty framework for our life in Christ, it is something we believe in, an object of faith. It is not, of course, on the same level as our faith in the Holy Trinity, but it is integral to and fully integrated in this faith. This corresponds to St. Cyprian's fundamental observation: "You cannot have God for your father unless you have the church for your mother" (*On the Unity of the Church*, 6). Even if this statement may originally have had certain "structural" implications, it clearly affirms that both theology and soteriology need an ecclesiological underpinning.

Directly translated, ecclesiology means "the doctrine of the church," and this means that the core of our present reflection must be the nature and purpose of the Church. Yet the task of ecclesiology cannot be reduced to producing some kind of institutional theory for the Church or the churches. Since the Church, in accordance with St. Cyprian, is the place or location both of salvation and of the life that stems from salvation, ecclesiology must rather be conceived as a perspective on Christian life in its totality.

Introduction: Ecumenical Ecclesiology?

Each communion or confession is fully entitled to reflect on the Church's nature on the basis of its own self-understanding. Moreover, since ecclesiology deals with a concrete reality and not with some kind of abstract idea, our denominational experiences are of considerable importance. Yet there are several reasons why ecclesiology is best done in community or within a wider ecumenical framework.[1] This holds true even if, or perhaps exactly because, ecclesiological problems are often described as the most difficult challenge today, ecumenically speaking. First, what is at stake here is basically the *una sancta*, the one Church of God, and not a multitude of parochial institutions. Second, since unity belongs to the Church's nature, reflections on this entity must also be as unified as possible. As a matter of fact, a vast number of disparate or narrow ecclesiologies effectively conceal the Church's unity. Third, it must be realized that denominational ecclesiologies often serve primarily the maintenance or self-perpetuation of parochial institutions at the cost of commitment to the *una sancta*. Accordingly, denominationally conditioned approaches may be seen as valid in this field only as denominationally conditioned approaches. For they are definitely not the whole story.[2]

What has been said so far applies particularly to the churches of the Reformation. This is not so much because of the gloomy fact that theological ecclesiology has actually never been a primary concern of most of these churches. It derives rather from what I have characterized as the regulative or reactive nature of the ecclesiological reflection of the Reformers. As indicated in Chapter 1, the Lutheran Reformers focused especially on the issues that they held to be in most immediate need of renewal in the contemporary Roman Catholic Church, while keeping significant and essential parts of Catholic ecclesiology. This was in consequence of the basic catholicity and ecumenicity of the authentic Reformation movement.

Seen in this perspective, it can even be argued that the Reformation never had a full ecclesiology or a complete ecclesiological system, at least not until there was a clear need to develop a kind of institutional

---

[1] An example of an effort to write ecclesiology from an ecumenical perspective can be found in George H. Tavard, *The Church, the Community of Salvation: An Ecumenical Ecclesiology* (Collegeville, Minn.: The Liturgical Press, 1992). See also my own attempt: *Kirken-troens mor: Et økumenisk bidrag til en økumenisk ekklesiologi* (Oslo: Verbum, 1999). In Carl H. Braaten, *Mother Church: Ecclesiology and Ecumenism* (Minneapolis: Fortress Press, 1998), there is a forceful defense of an ecumenical approach to ecclesiology. Let me also refer to a recent Faith and Order text at this point: *The Nature and Purpose of the Church: A Stage on the Way to a Common Statement*, Faith and Order Paper No. 181 (Geneva: World Council of Churches, 1998).

[2] Basically, this can be seen as corresponding with Edmund Schlink's distinction between fundamental *Heilsgeschichtliche* ecclesiological structures of lasting theological importance and denominationally conditioned structures. See his *Ökumenische Dogmatik: Grundzüge* (Göttingen: Vandenhoeck & Ruprecht, 1983) especially 558ff.

theory for parochial, regional or national church institutions over against the "universal" Roman Catholic Church. As already indicated, the Roman Catholic understanding of the Church emerges as the most appropriate framework, perhaps even the only appropriate framework, for our interpretation of the ecclesiological reflection of the Reformers, despite their criticisms of aspects of Roman practice.[3] Today this clearly directs us toward an ecumenical way of doing ecclesiology.

What, then, *is* ecumenical ecclesiology? Let me first mention that the point here is not merely to compare different ecclesiologies. That enterprise and its corresponding "sociologization" of ecclesiology are, in my view, of limited relevance. Moreover, the goal of an ecumenical approach to ecclesiology is definitely not only to locate a tiny and neat center or a least common denominator that allows us to maintain divergent denominational ecclesiologies and identities. Nor is the goal to achieve total uniformity or standardization. Quite the contrary, ecumenical ecclesiological reflection is directed toward the immense richness of the witness and the experience of the Church that has taken place within God's people from its beginning and in all parts of the world. At this point it holds true that ecumenism is supposed to make us richer and not poorer. The key challenge is to encompass this richness in a "system" in which diverging positions are led into a convergence. This, moreover, involves a dialectic between enriching diversity and commitment to unity.

In this connection, Holy Scripture plays a decisive authoritative role, but clearly not in the sense that all answers are given once and for all in the Bible. The Scriptures rather present the point of departure for the dynamic process of God's dealing with his people. This means that ecumenical ecclesiology should be based on an interaction between the Word of God and its "effects" throughout the history of the Church. And while denominational ecclesiologies tend to become parochial and minimalist, an ecumenical approach is the best way to reflect the vast richness of the life of the Church. An ecumenically based ecclesiol-

---

[3] Let me add that the best ecclesiological literature in my view stems from Roman Catholic authors, while this has often been a conspicuously poor literary genre among Protestants. Contributions like Henri de Lubac, *The Splendour of the Church* (London: Sheed and Ward, 1956); idem, *The Motherhood of the Church* (San Francisco: Ignatius Press, 1982); and Louis Bouyer, *The Church of God: Body of Christ and Temple of the Spirit* (Chicago: Franciscan Herald Press, 1982) have had an immense impact on my own reflections. A major study, with an English summary, of de Lubac's ecclesiology is Peter Bexell, *Kyrkan som Sacrament: Henri de Lubacs fundamentalecklesiology* (Stockholm: Brutus Östlings Bokförlag, 1997).

ogy can be characterized as our common return to the one and undivided Church as well as a common openness towards God's future.

Finally, recent ecclesiological debates have taught us that the Church must be seen from "below" as well as from "above." The Church is both a divine reality and a servant or instrument of the genuinely human desire for community. The challenge is to hold these two perspectives together. For while the *von oben* church can only be found in its *von unten* shape, there can be no *von unten* church that is not firmly grounded in God's work through Christ in the Holy Spirit. This calls for an incarnational approach to ecclesiology in which we aim at keeping divine and human aspects together without falsely confusing them. Such an approach in turn prompts us toward a vision of the Church as a spiritual as well as a truly earthly entity, or, put differently, the mother of faith and the priest of creation. Ecumenical ecclesiology, therefore, also aims at accounting for the role of the Church in God's world.

The Church as the Body of Christ and Christ's Sacrament to Us—Christological Foundation and Sacramental Implications

In the Scriptures the Church is described as anchored in the work and life of the Holy Trinity. First, it is *the people of God*. This image echoes the Church's dynamic nature as a pilgrim people, being always ready to go when its Lord calls. Moreover, it points toward the Church's continuity with the people of Israel of the old covenant (Rom 9:25ff.). However, God's new people is open to all and is not limited to a particular group or ethnicity (1 Pet 2:10). Second, it is *the body of Christ*. This image will be discussed in more detail later, but it should be noted here that several other images reflect the christological foundation of the Church. This is the case with the picture of the tree and the branches (John 15:5), the portrayal of Christ as the cornerstone of the edifice (Eph 2:20-22), and the description of the Church as Christ's bride (Rev 19:7 and 21:1ff.). Third, it is *the temple of the Holy Spirit* (1 Pet 2:4ff.) and a dwelling-place of the Spirit (Eph 2:20ff.). In light of this, one may say that the church of the New Testament has a charismatic nature in the sense that the gifts of grace are supposed to build up the Church as a whole.[4]

---

[4] Concerning New Testament ecclesiology in general, I would particularly like to refer to some essential contributions by Gerhard Lohfink: *Jesus and Community: the Social Dimension of Christian Faith* (Philadelphia: Fortress Press; New York/Ramsey: Paulist

Now, all these aspects belong to a full ecclesiology. If one of them is played down or neglected, the result will be a one-sided or clearly deficient perception of the Church. Actually, the need for *all* the elements of a trinitarian ecclesiology is affirmed by the fact that these elements are interconnected. As will be seen, this is particularly the case with regard to the christological and pneumatological dimensions, reflected in the fact that the Spirit plays a crucial role in the Church's existence as the Body of Christ. Moreover, God's church is Christ's church and vice versa. Nevertheless, a trinitarian ecclesiology has a core, and this core is the Church's christological foundation. In the New Testament this seems to be the case both quantitatively and qualitatively. This concern can be and has been emphasized in a misleading way, for instance, when a christologically grounded ecclesiology is confused with massive institutionalism. But surely, occasional misuse should not be allowed to cut us off from this basic aspect of New Testament ecclesiology.

Furthermore, when we speak of a christological foundation, it is not necessarily implied that the Church was instituted by a single direct act of the earthly Jesus. The Church in its fullness presupposes both the risen Christ and the sending of the Holy Spirit. Yet there can be little doubt that Christ's work on earth and the church are clearly interrelated; indeed, with Leonhard Goppelt one can even claim that his work necessarily points beyond itself toward the existence of the Church.[5] For it was his task to collect a messianic people, and not only to preach abstract ideas. Alfred Loisy's ecclesiologically speaking fatal insistence that "Jesus preached the Kingdom of God while it was the church that came" calls for substantial correction. The same is the case with the idea that Jesus' eschatological message gradually was swapped for a church-focused *Frühkatholizismus,* or the early Catholicism of the catholic letters of the New Testament.

Trying to clarify what a christologically based ecclesiology means in concrete terms, St. Paul's forceful presentation of the contents and

---

Press, 1984), and *Braucht Gott die Kirche? Zur Theologie des Volkes Gottes* (Freiburg : Herder, 1998). See further Yves Congar, *Das Mysterium des Tempels: Die Geschichte des Gegenwart Gottes von der Genesis bis zur Apokalypse* (Salzburg: Otto Müller, 1960), and the classic account of Rudolf Schnackenburg, *The Church in the New Testament* (London: Burns and Oates, 1974).

[5] See Leonhard Goppelt, *Theologie des Neuen Testaments,* vol. 1 (Göttingen: Vandenhoeck & Ruprecht, 1975) 254ff.

implications of the image of the Church as a body, or more accurately as Christ's body, in 1 Corinthians 12 is of fundamental significance. We cannot go into this rich account in detail, but some observations are particularly important here:

1) When St. Paul reminds the Corinthians that "you are the body of Christ and individually members of it" (1 Cor 12:27), the point is not that the church in Corinth in happy moments may resemble Christ's body, but rather that it *is* that body. Without claiming that this is an expression of total identification, it nevertheless seems clear that the Church in this verse is understood both as belonging to the Lord and as a most specific and transparent representation in the world of the dead and risen Christ.

2) Seen in connection with the two previous chapters of 1 Corinthians, there is much evidence here that the Church becomes Christ's body when the faithful eat his flesh and drink his blood in the Eucharist (see especially 1 Cor 10:16ff. and 11:26). This means that the body image is eucharistically grounded and that the Church's identity as the body of Christ is manifested most clearly when we celebrate the Eucharist.

3) Within Christ's body, each member is called to contribute to the growth of the body as a whole and to the common good. This affirms the social or communal nature of life in Christ, and it corresponds with the assertion that love is a bond that "binds everything together in perfect harmony" (Col 3:14).

4) Within the body of Christ, "there are varieties of gifts, but the same Spirit" (1 Cor.12:4), a clear implication that it is the unifying work of the Holy Spirit that keeps the one body together. Accordingly, the image of the body of Christ explicitly includes pneumatology; it is meaningless to pit a christologically based and a pneumatologically focused ecclesiology against each other.

5) In Ephesians and Colossians we encounter another version of the body image when Christ is described as the head of the body (see Eph 4:15ff. and Col 1:18). The cosmic range and eschatological nature of the Church are stressed: "he has put all things under his feet and has made him the head over all things for the church, which is his body, the fullness of him who fills all in all" (Eph 1:22-23).

In the final analysis, the most important argument in favor of a christologically based ecclesiology is the simple fact that without the work of Christ, without his death and resurrection, there would be no new people of God and no church. Moreover, the fruits of his sacrifice are made available and become ours precisely in the Church. The

Church, to be sure, has a divine as well as a human nature, and its human dimension includes an awareness that it is also marked by the brokenness of human life. This, however, does not in any sense exclude or block Christ's presence in the Church, for he who was incarnate as a human being and became our brother can also be incarnate in the Church. This does not necessarily imply that the Church should be described as a kind of "extension of the incarnation," although the incarnation event emerges as both the theological foundation of, and the model for, Christ's continued presence in the Church. Here one may even apply the term "sacrament of incarnation."

As we address some of the questions that concern the sacramentality or the sacramental character of the Church, what has been said so far about Christ's presence in the Church must be the starting point. We have already noted that this presence is most real and concrete. In accordance with the doctrine of Christ's *ubiquity,* he who fills everything in everyone is also fully capable of being everywhere, even when he is seated at the right hand of the Father, for the whole cosmos is filled with his glory. This rules out a merely spiritual, internal, or abstract presence. The presence of Christ in the Church, however, is not "immediate"; it is rather a *mediated* one. And it is mediated through specific means, namely, the means of grace or word and sacrament. These means can properly be described as the backbone of the Church. This definitely does not imply that Christ's presence in the Church is less real, for the means or signs that mediate his presence are concrete and empirically recognizable and thus "really real." Moreover, when we pray the *Agnus Dei,* the prayer is just as much directed to Christ at the altar, the one who comes to us through the gifts of bread and wine, as to Christ in heaven. In this perspective, a christologically based ecclesiology points directly toward the means of grace and also toward a sacramentally grounded approach to the Church.

Word and sacrament constitute the Church. The key point here, however, is not that these factors are juridically decisive for the Church as institution, but rather that they mediate the presence of Christ, without which no true church can exist. The Word of God, always consisting of gospel as well as law, calls us to the new life in Christ that is lived in the Church (see Rom 10:13ff.). Baptism, the *prima porta gratiae et ecclesiae* ("the first gate to grace and the church"), implies concrete participation in Christ, or more precisely concrete participation in his death and resurrection (Rom 6). Moreover, we are baptized into the one body of the Church, and so baptism has a fundamental ecclesiological significance. Penitence or confession can be construed as a continual or daily return to the grace of baptism. Further, in the Eucharist we become Christ's body by eating his flesh and drinking his blood (see 1 Cor 10:16ff.). It can be argued that the Eucharist in a particular way manifests or even "makes" the Church.[6] All these means, being empirically recognizable, also visualize the Church. We will return both to the individual sacraments and to the question of the number of sacramental acts later on. However, already at this stage it can be concluded that word and sacrament are to be described as the backbone of the body of the Church simply because they mediate the concrete participation in Christ that is at the core of the church's life. Thus there is much evidence that not only liturgical worship but also the office of the ministry that is responsible for the public administration of the means of grace are implicitly church constitutive in providing the essential framework for word and sacrament.

Generally speaking, the Lutheran Reformers' theology of the means of grace does not seem to exclude a sacramental ecclesiology. Admittedly, their favored approach is to see the Church as *creatura verbi*—as an entity that is created by God's word and that has the same word as its most eminent mark. The question is, however, whether the notion of *creatura verbi* should be seen in contrast to a sacramental perception. For there was a strong awareness of the interaction between word and sacrament among the Reformers, an awareness normally associated with their acceptance of St. Augustine's insistence that the sacrament should be understood as *verbum visibile*, a "visible word." However, this approach can also be turned the other way around: by their stress on the essentially outward nature and the immediate efficacy of God's word as a word that "creates what it names" (N.F.S. Grundtvig), one could argue that the Reformers came close to a basically sacramental understanding of the word. In the final analysis, the theological differences between a Catholic account of the sacraments and Lutheran deliberations on the word often appear to be limited or quite modest.

Still, Lutheran—or Protestant—theologians have been quite reluctant to describe the Church in sacramental terms.[7] This reluctance was

---

[6] On the interconnection between the Eucharist and the Church, see the fascinating account in Paul McPartlan, *The Eucharist Makes the Church: Henri de Lubac and John Zizioulas in Dialogue* (Edinburgh: T&T Clark, 1993).

[7] See Eberhard Jüngel, "Die Kirche als Sakrament?" *Zeitschrift für systematische Theologie* 80 (1983) 432ff. However, and as a curiosity, it can be mentioned that the liberal

doubtlessly relevant in view of the Romantic proclivity, for instance within the so-called Tübingen school, to identify Christ and the Church in a false way, almost to the point that the Church took Christ's place. In several cases this position inevitably led to dense institutionalism and ecclesiocentrism. There is also much evidence that the use of the term *Ursakrament* ("basic or original sacrament") concerning the Church was problematic; in the final instance, only Christ can be the *Ursakrament.* But these positions belong to the past; they go back one-hundred-fifty and fifty years respectively. Today the main problem is not that Christ and the Church are being falsely identified, but rather the opposite: they are often torn totally apart, not least by the insistence that "Jesus is okay, but the church is hopeless." Against this background, the task today is to say something about the essential connection between Christ and the Church that is his body. And this includes an awareness that our life in Christ is lived in the Church.

To explore this a bit further, an important statement by Henri de Lubac offers an appropriate point of departure: "If Christ is God's sacrament, then the church is Christ's sacrament to us. For it represents him in the whole ancient force of this term by making him truly present."[8] The Church is "Christ's sacrament to us"; there clearly is both a difference and an interconnection between Christ and the Church. On the one hand, the difference is that only Christ can be seen as the *source* of salvation, while the Church is its *instrument.* Accordingly, sacramentality should be perceived as instrumentality, an essential instrument of salvation. On the other hand, however, the interconnection between Christ and the Church consists in Christ being fully and truly present in the Church, which implies that the church is the place of salvation.

The fundamental starting point that is provided by de Lubac can be supplemented in two ways: first, by alluding to St. Cyprian's insistence that the Church is the *sacramentum unitatis* ("the sacrament of unity"). This signifies that the Church is the place where unity in Christ is lived and also that it emerges as a sign of unity for the world. Sec-

---

theologian Rudolf Sohm insisted that "the sacrament of the incarnation repeats itself in the sacrament of the church," in his "Das altkatholische Kirchenrecht und das Dekret Gratians," in *Festschrift der Leipziger Juristenfakultät für Dr. Adolf Wach* (Munich, 1918) 83. Within ecumenical dialogues, a new openness to a sacramentally based ecclesiology can be found. See, for example, *Die Sakramentalität der Kirche in der ökumenischen Diskussion* (Paderborn: Bonifatius-Verlag, 1983).

[8] See Henri de Lubac, *Catholicisme: Les aspects sociaux du dogme* (Paris: Cerf, 1938) 45 (my translation).

ond, in a well-known phrase that often is associated with Karl Rahner, the Church is described as *sacramentum mundi,* a sacrament in and for the world. An essentially dynamic dimension is added to the concept of sacramentality by pointing toward the Church's task and purpose to be the priest of creation and the first fruit of a reunited humankind.[9]

To summarize concretely what, in my view, a sacramentally grounded ecclesiology means, the following concerns play a key role: (1) What is primarily at stake is the conviction that the risen Christ is fully and truly present in his church. We are in Christ because Christ is in us. This is the core of sacramental theology. And our existence in Christ is realized within his body on earth, that is, the Church. (2) The Church is a sacramental sign, obviously not of itself, but rather of our salvation in Christ. The sacramentality of the Church immediately points toward its instrumentality. (3) A sacrament is not to be understood as an institutional building block, but rather as a sign and expression of the mystery of faith as this mystery is revealed in the Church. (4) The Church *is* a sacrament because it *has* sacraments and vice versa. This means that the key manifestation of the Church's sacramentality is its administration and celebration of the sacramental acts that encompass all of life, be they two, three, or seven. (5) The Church is a sign of the fulfillment of God's kingdom. Since this includes the vision of a redeemed creation and a reunited humankind, the Church is a sacrament in and for the world. All these points, as well as the sacramental concept as such, prompt us to view the Church as the place of salvation.

The Church as the Place of Salvation: On Church and Justification

Turning more explicitly to the Church's role in the drama of salvation, there are two ditches that must be avoided. On the one hand, we have the tendency totally to identify Christ and the Church, for instance, by describing the Church as *Heilsanstalt* ("the institution of salvation") in a manner that implies that the Church almost takes Christ's place. As already indicated, views like this can be found, among others, within

---

[9] Karl Rahner, *The Church and the Sacraments* (New York: Herder and Herder; London: Burns and Oates, 1963). A similar approach is advocated by Edward Schillebeeckx in *World and Church* (London: Sheed and Ward, 1971). I am aware that de Lubac was not totally convinced by Rahner's and Schillebeeckx's approaches at this point, but this does not seem to rule out the possibility of seeing these approaches together.

the Roman Catholic Tübingen school at the middle of the nineteenth century. On the other hand, we have the Protestant proclivity to tear Christ and the Church, and therefore salvation and the Church, totally apart. This position is reflected when liberal-pietists insist that the church can best be seen as a purely practical framework for our faith life; at worst it emerges as an impediment to authentic personal religiosity. Such a perception is also possibly based on a purely forensic interpretation of justification in which the event of justification is reduced to an abstract idea that has no need for a concrete framework.[10]

In trying to locate an intermediate position between these two extremes, my proposal is that we speak about the Church as the *place* or *location* of salvation. For the fact is that salvation does not take place in some kind of abstract or personalized vacuum, but rather in the concrete space of the Church. This approach corresponds to the view of the Church as the instrument of salvation even as it moves beyond a purely functional interpretation of instrumentality. I cannot enter the debates on the relationships between church and salvation and church and justification in detail; I shall therefore have to limit myself to the following observations.[11]

1) Justification in Christ by grace through faith must be seen as theologically prior to ecclesiology. The Church is a sign of and a service to the gospel of justification, and not the other way around. Moreover, the doctrine of justification can be described as the *articulus stantis et cadentis ecclesiae* ("the article by which the church stands and falls"), simply in the sense that without justification in Christ, there would be no new people of God and thus no church. At the same time, it must be emphasized that the personal appropriation of salvation takes place in

[10] I cannot go into the long and intense debates on the forensic and effective aspects of justification here. However, among liberal-pietists there has been a tendency to ignore Christ's work *in nobis*, reducing the valid "come as you are" principle to a most static "remain as you always have been" idea. Accordingly, one may argue that in these circles the emphasis on Christian life and on a dynamic growth in this life occasionally comes close to disappearing. When the challenge of an ever more committed life in Christ is somehow marginalized, there will presumably also be a proclivity to neglect the place where this life is lived, namely, the Church. This emerges as another consequence of an abstract and isolated understanding of justification.

[11] The points mentioned here are largely taken from my article "The Church as the Place of Salvation: On the Interrelation Between Justification and Ecclesiology," *Pro Ecclesia* 9 (2000) 285ff. In that essay my position is developed somewhat more comprehensively, partly with a view to the Roman Catholic–Lutheran *Joint Declaration on the Doctrine of Justification* (Grand Rapids: Eerdmans, 1999).

the Church through the means of grace. Accordingly, soteriology and ecclesiology can be distinguished, but they can definitely not be completely torn apart.

2) In ecumenical debates, there is often a focus on what are termed "ecclesiological consequences of the doctrine of justification." Such consequences do exist, but as far as I can see, they pertain more to the Church's service and mission—the Church being called to stand forth in the world as a body of justified and liberated sinners—than to its structural shape and essential nature. It is counterproductive when the doctrine of justification is held to be the only structuring, or rather destructuring, principle in the Church's life. The same is the case with the proclivity to argue that the ecclesiological significance of the doctrine of justification by and large is that there is no ecclesiology.

3) Subsequent to this, it must be emphasized that the doctrine of justification tends to degenerate into an abstract theory and loses its liberating power when it is isolated and its trinitarian foundation in the faith of the Church as a whole neglected. Minimalist or reductionist approaches to justification must be rejected. Justification can only function as the hermeneutical center of theology when it is the center of *something*, and not when it is placed in splendid isolation and even played off against the fullness of the Church's witness throughout history. Moreover, it is only Christ who can justify sinners, not a *doctrine* of justification. The isolated or almost hypostatic approach to justification that seems to be preeminent among liberal-pietist Protestants is theologically misleading.

4) Jesus Christ is the chief link between justification and the Church, salvation and ecclesiology. He is the one who justifies, and the Church is his body. When the Church is seen as Christ's body, a role in the process of salvation must be attributed to it. On the other hand, when this christological approach is missing or dismissed, the Church's task in mediating salvation tends also to be forgotten. As we have seen, this is the main problem with the ecclesiology of liberal-pietistic Protestantism, a problem that points toward ecclesiological minimalism or pure pragmatism.

5) Christ's saving presence in the Church is mediated by the Holy Spirit through word and sacrament. This means that it is not the ecclesial institution as such that is soteriologically relevant, but rather the Church as the place where, through the means of grace, we participate in Christ's sacrificial offering. Accordingly, the Church's role in the appropriation of salvation becomes particularly transparent in its

worship, with a special emphasis on the celebration of the Eucharist as our concrete sacramental "memorial" of Christ's sacrifice. In this light, liturgy emerges as an effective "re-presentation" of the central events of salvation.

6) What has been said thus far is largely in correspondence with the vital Article V of the Augsburg Confession (AC). The following concerns are particularly important here: (a) Already in the initial words of AC Article V, it is stated that in order to obtain the faith that is a prerequisite of justification, God has instituted the office of the ordained ministry as a service to word and sacrament in the Church, a clear affirmation of the interaction between ecclesiology and soteriology. (b) Through these means of grace, the Holy Spirit is given and works faith in us, an indication that our participation in the fruits of Christ's offering is realized through word and sacrament. (c) The means of grace do not float around freely but are available only in the space of the church, where they are administered by the ordained ministry within the framework of liturgical worship. (d) The *ubi et quando visum est Deo* (" when and where God pleases") of AC Article V underlines God's freedom in giving salvation. Yet we are not God, and from our viewpoint the rule is that the giving of salvation takes place through word and sacrament in the Church. (e) In this light, the condemnation in AC Article V of "the Anabaptists" for denying that the Spirit comes to us through outward means can actually be understood as an indictment of all efforts to tear salvation and the Church apart.

7) In the Church's life, justification is mediated through all the means of grace which have the gospel as their core. Yet there is much evidence that the drama of justification is expressed or communicated in a particularly direct manner in the celebration of the Eucharist. This is because of the intimate relationship between the sacrament of the altar and the sacrifice of Christ that is the foundation of our justification. On the one hand, this sacrifice took place once and for all at Calvary, which means that it neither requires repetition nor can it be repeated. On the other hand, the sacrifice of the cross should not be reduced to an isolated point in history, for every time we gather around the eucharistic table in remembrance of our Lord, his offering is made sacramentally and effectively present.

8) Being justified sinners, all stand on the same level before God, and this excludes the possibility of an ontologically founded hierarchy in the Church. Yet Christ's body requires an appropriate division of labor to express its nature and facilitate its mission. Moreover, the fact

that the doctrine of justification is explicitly linked in AC Article V to the service of the ordained ministry affirms that this doctrine does not in any sense exclude such a distribution of duties, the setting apart of specific persons to take care of specific tasks in the Church's life. Quite the contrary, the service of the Church's ministry in its different forms is essential to the mediation of salvation in Christ. This corresponds to Melanchthon's insistence in Article VII of the Apology that the ordained ministry can be seen as a representation of Christ.

9) Christ also liberates those who are justified by grace from self-centeredness and meanness, empowering them to live at peace with God and their fellow human beings. As the community of the justified, the Church is called to embody the good news that forgiveness is a gift to be received from God and shared with others. Such a church has the capacity to serve as a sign of generosity, solidarity, and reconciliation in a world that desperately needs but acutely lacks such deeds, an affirmation of its existence and calling as *sacramentum mundi.*

10) For Martin Luther, the emphasis on the outward and empirically recognizable means of grace as administered in the space of the Church was not only of significance as a kind of ecclesiological "theory" but also as a comfort for the troubled soul. In opposition to the so-called Enthusiasts, who focused on the inward effects of the Spirit, Luther argued: "If now I seek the forgiveness of sins, I do not run to the cross, for I will not find it given there. Nor must I hold to the suffering of Christ . . . in knowledge or remembrance, for I will not find it there either. But I will find in the sacrament or gospel the word which distributes, presents, offers, and gives to me that forgiveness which was won on the cross."[12] Against this background, one may suggest that in the final analysis contemporary liberal-pietists have more in common with the Enthusiasts than with Martin Luther.

In concluding this account of the connection between church and justification, I would like to briefly emphasize three crucial concerns. (1) Without being grounded in Christ and his work, the doctrine of justification becomes void and empty. (2) If it is not rooted in the reality of the Church, this doctrine will degenerate to an abstract theory. (3) Salvation is life in its fullness and not just some kind of private or internal event or an adherence to a specific set of beliefs. Seen in this way, our new existence as justified sinners requires a concrete space or location,

---

[12] Martin Luther, *Against the Heavenly Prophets* (1525), *Luther's Works* 40 (Philadelphia: Fortress Press, 1958) 214.

namely, the Church. Being the place where faith is born, nourished, and lived on the basis of our *koinonia* with the Father through the Son in the Holy Spirit, the Church becomes not the source but the locus of salvation. This is where salvation becomes ours through word and sacrament. So there is a fundamental interaction between justification and the Church, soteriology and ecclesiology. If this interaction is ignored, there will be negative repercussions not only for ecclesiology but also for soteriology and Christology.

Now, some may find the picture of the Church that has been conveyed in these reflections idealistic and out of touch with the at least occasionally quite gloomy ecclesial realities. I can see that point. Often the failures that stem from the Church's "human form" become far more visible than its "divine origin." And I would be the first to admit that a church that repeatedly falls short of its calling is a most discouraging thing. Yet I will continue to insist that the Church also can be the opposite: it can actually be heartbreakingly beautiful. This is so, quite simply, because the Church is a celebration of the most beautiful thing that can be envisioned: the One who gives his life for the many. Since this event is the basis of our justification, the old saying *extra ecclesiam nulla salus est* ("there is no salvation outside the church") actually holds true. For even if soteriology and ecclesiology cannot be treated as totally overlapping entities, it is in the space of the Church that Christ's righteousness becomes ours. This makes it appropriate to repeat once more the crucial and highly pertinent ecclesiological affirmation of St. Cyprian: "You cannot have God for your father unless you have the church for your mother" (*On the Unity of the Church*, 6).

A Structured People—On the Ministries of the Church

The most appropriate framework for addressing the many questions that relate to the ordained ministry is not the—in itself—fully legitimate requirement of structures and "order."[13] Rather, what is at

---

[13] From the vast literature on the Church's ministry, I will limit myself to a few references: Regin Prenter, *Kirkens embete: Udkast til en det kirkelige embetes dogmatik med luthersk udgangspunkt* (Aarhus: Universitetsforlaget, 1965); Edward Schillebeeckx, *Ministry: Leadership in the Community of Jesus Christ* (New York: Crossroad, 1984); and Karl Rahner, *Vorfragen zu einem ökumenischen Amtsverständnis* (Freiburg: Herder, 1974). Among several ecumenical texts, the relevant parts of Faith and Order's so-called Lima text, *Baptism, Eucharist and Ministry*, Faith and Order Paper No. 111 (Geneva: World Council of Churches, 1982), plays a particularly important role. See also the Roman Catholic-Lutheran Joint Commission, *The Ministry in the Church* (Geneva: Lutheran World Federation, 1981).

stake is the desperate need of a functioning spiritual leadership in the Church. This need was also expressed by Jesus in his reaction when he saw the crowds: "He had compassion for them, because they were harassed and helpless, like sheep without a shepherd" (Matt 9:36). While such leadership appears to be more and more difficult to exercise in today's world, it remains fundamental in view of the nature as well as the mission of the Church. A church that has lost such a leadership is radically weakened, regardless of how affluent it may be in terms of material resources. At the same time, a church that possesses appropriate spiritual leadership can be immensely strong even if it lacks such resources. It is therefore crucial to provide for the exercise of leadership within the whole people of God through specially commissioned leaders. And while several approaches may be feasible, it is the form of personal commitment embedded in a personally exercised leadership that is of crucial significance in the Church's life.

Models for this service can, of course, be found in Holy Scripture. However, it is clear that in this area the Bible only reflects the first stages of a dynamic development. As the early Church grew, the need to create new forms of leadership became evident. This was particularly the case with regard to the emerging episcopal ministry, a ministry actually not necessary before the apostles had passed away or before there were several churches in the same location. The evolving structures of the early Church are also vital for us today.

The following reflections will focus on the so-called public ministries of the Church or, better put, on the office of the ministry. For this office the act of ordination, in which several central ministerial concerns are gathered, is of essential significance. Ordination is, first, an expression of the fact that God is the one who authorizes and equips the ordinand. The ordination act must be seen primarily in a vertical perspective, as a mediation of the charism of leadership. Liturgically, this is reflected through an *epiklesis*, the invocation of the Holy Spirit, which is fundamental to all acts of ordination or initiation.

Second, within such a framework ordination can and should be understood in sacramental terms; it includes a special promise from God as well as the "external" act of prayer and the laying on of hands. Melanchthon, in Article XIII of the Apology, was prepared to describe ordination as a sacrament.

Third, however, the act of ordination also includes a more horizontal perspective in the sense that it conveys and to a certain degree presupposes the calling of all the faithful. Accordingly, the ordained minister stands both in the middle of and over against the whole people, belonging to the fellowship of all baptized believers and at the same time exercising a special form of authority toward this fellowship.

Fourth, we have already noted that it was the conviction of the Lutheran Reformers, as expressed in Article XIV of the Augsburg Confession, that only those who are "properly called" or ordained may officiate with word and sacrament, thus excluding so-called lay eucharistic presidency. However, the intention of this is definitely not to establish the means of grace as the "private property" of the ministers, but on the contrary to demonstrate that those who are ordained to the public ministry are supposed to prevent things that belong to all the faithful from being monopolized or annexed by individuals or special groups.

Fifth, without necessarily conveying a special "character" *(character indelebilis)* to the ordinand, ordination represents the start of a life-long ministry. It also entails inclusion in the college of priests across time and space.

Within post-Reformation Lutheranism there has been a strong emphasis on the "oneness" of the ministry of the Church, even if the original Lutheran confessions seem to contain no theologically binding affirmation of this ministerial oneness. Clearly, everything that belongs to and derives from the Church's ministry must be firmly fixed in that which constitutes the Church, word and sacrament. In this sense, one may here speak theologically of a fundamental "oneness." However, this should not be confused with structural standardization; and, moreover, theological oneness does not exclude a certain differentiation. This also appears to be confirmed by the pattern that has been adopted by most Lutheran churches—not having one but several public ministries—as well as by AC Article XXVIII, which expresses a clear wish to keep the episcopal office. The key concern is to find a structure that serves the Church's nature and mission in the best way. This would seem to require a measure of ministerial diversity and suggests, furthermore, that the so-called threefold ministry—deacon, priest, and bishop—still is viable. This pattern is reflected in the New Testament and in the ancient Church; it has ample support in recent ecumenical documents (for example, Faith and Order's important Lima statement of 1982, *Baptism, Eucharist and Ministry)*, and it has throughout the history of the Church provided an appropriate framework for mission.

Within this threefold structure, the office of the priest or pastor (the difference between these two terms should not be exaggerated) is theologically highly significant. This depends on the fact that this office, firmly anchored in the liturgical life of the Church, is most directly embedded in the constitutive service of word and sacrament. Seen in light of AC Articles V and XIV, the priestly or pastoral office is essential to the administration of the means of grace, and therefore essential to the church as a whole. Accordingly, it can be argued that the ordained ministry belongs implicitly to the constitutive factors of the church that are listed in AC Article VII. Furthermore, as expressed most directly in the German version of AC Article V, the church's ministry *(ministerium ecclesiasticum)* is instituted by God. And, as we have pointed out earlier, Melanchthon in Article VII of the Apology specifically indicates that "those who hold office in the church" represent Christ. In serving the faithful with word and sacrament, the priest or the pastor truly acts *in persona Christi,* of course without being identical to Christ. At the same time, the priestly office also has a pneumatological dimension, in the sense that it is based on a particular ministerial charism and carried out in the power of the Holy Spirit. All this leads to the conclusion that the office of the ministry must be seen in a comprehensive trinitarian perspective. Jerome's statement that "there is no church without priests" *(ecclesia non est quae non habet sacerdotes)* rings true. The priestly or pastoral ministry is clearly essential to the Church's life.

The office of the bishop is essential in providing proper ecclesial leadership and exercising oversight and authority.[14] This is based on the fact that the bishop has a special place and role in the whole Church's *successio apostolica:* to represent the apostles by guarding apostolic doctrine or tradition, in community with the priests and the faithful as a whole. This succession does not imply a repetition of the ministry of the first apostles, but an essential continuation of that ministry and its basic intentions. Bishops also function as vital signs of unity and continuity in the Church. They represent the local churches universally and the universal Church locally, thus providing an effective bond of unity, as was particularly clear in the early Church. From a human point of view, there are serious reasons to doubt that the Church would have survived as one without the collegial and conciliar fellowship of bishops. Today the existence of several parallel or even competing local bishoprics represents a challenge when it comes to regaining

[14] On the episcopal office, see among others *Episcopal Ministry: The Report of the Archbishop's Group on the Episcopate* (London: Church House Publishing, 1990); Hervé Legrand and Christoph Theobalds, eds., *Le ministère des évêques au concile Vatican II et depuis* (Paris: Cerf, 2001); Peter Moore, ed., *Bishops—But What Kind?* (London: SPCK, 1982).

the unity of the episcopate. A unified episcopate clearly belongs to ecclesial communion. However, if this unity cannot be expressed personally, the possibility of a collegial model could be considered at least in
the initial stages of such communion.[15] Finally, the bishop's responsibility for, and service to, unity is expressed in a most lucid manner
when the bishop celebrates the Eucharist together with the priests in
the midst of the faithful, preferably in the diocesan cathedral. This also
reflects the essential pastoral nature of the episcopal office; the bishop
is to be far more than a church administrator.

According to the New Testament, the Church is local and universal. While the priestly office serves the local church and the bishop provides a link between the local and the universal levels, there is much
reason to believe that we also need some kind of universal ministry in
order to express and guard the Church's essential universality. This
has traditionally been the task of the Bishop of Rome.[16] We cannot go
into all the questions that relate to the papal office here, but it should
be mentioned briefly that the main problem at this point, as I see it, is
not infallibility. That doctrine can be seen as grounded in God's promise to the Church in the Holy Spirit and his corresponding assurance
that we shall remain in the truth. Infallibility thus emerges as an integral part of authoritative teaching; it applies to the few formal *ex cathe-
dra* pronouncements of the pope, in which he defines issues of faith on
behalf of the whole Church.

A more difficult issue in regard to the papal office is perhaps the
matter of "universal jurisdiction." On the one hand, the universality of
the church requires some kind of universal authority. On the other
hand, the subtle balance between unity and diversity suggests that
such jurisdiction always must be exercised within a collegial and communal framework in which the whole college of bishops plays a cru-

---

[15] Interestingly, a similar suggestion has been made by Pierre Duprey, formerly of
the Vatican's Secretariat for Christian Unity, in "The Unity We Seek," in C. S. Song, ed.,
Growing Together into Unity: Texts of the Faith and Order Commission on Conciliar Fellowship
(Geneva and Madras: World Council of Churches, 1978) 127ff.

[16] With regard to the papal office, Pope John Paul II's encyclical *Ut unum sint* (1995)
is of crucial importance. See also Carl E. Braaten and Robert W. Jenson, eds., *Church
Unity and the Papal Office: An Ecumenical Dialogue on John Paul II's Encyclical* Ut Unum Sint
(Grand Rapids: Eerdmans, 2001); James F. Puglisi, ed., *Petrine Ministry and the Unity of
the Church: Toward a Patient and Fraternal Dialogue* (Collegeville, Minn.: The Liturgical
Press, 1999); and *The Gift of Authority: Authority in the Church III,* An Agreed Statement
by the Second Anglican-Roman Catholic International Commission (London: Catholic
Truth Society; Toronto: Anglican Book Centre; New York: Church Publishing, Inc., 1999).

cial role. In practical terms, collegiality can be realized both through synods and through the principle of subsidiarity, which means that decisions in most cases should be taken at the lowest possible level in the Church's life.

Concerning the diaconate, I can express only one concern: this ministry should be perceived neither as a purely charitable or social service nor as mere preparation for the priestly office. The distinct feature of the diaconate is rather that it is a link between *leitourgia* and *diakonia,* between liturgical worship and service in the world. Such a link is absolutely fundamental to the nature and mission of the Church, and it needs to be expressed and manifested through a particular ministry. In more concrete terms, the diaconate can be seen as being based in the offertory of the Eucharist. The deacon carries our offerings to the altar together with the gifts of bread and wine. Subsequently, from the eucharistic table we are sent out to the world to share our bread with those who hunger. This is clearly the responsibility of all the faithful, but the deacon is the one who leads the way from the Eucharist to the world and coordinates our efforts in this respect.[17]

Finally, a brief word is also necessary concerning the so-called common priesthood, or better, the priesthood of all baptized believers, in relation to the ordained ministries of the Church.[18] On the one hand, the priesthood of all the baptized is of essential significance in the life of the Church. This priesthood must be seen as a participation in the priestly office of Christ, and as such it is an indication that mediating institutions like the Old Testament high priest are no longer necessary when the believer turns to God. In Christ the way to God is open to all. On the other hand, as important as this concern may be, it tends to become blurred when it is confused with the ordained ministries. Here an appropriate division of labor is needed. Further, the priesthood of all believers cannot be used as an argument in favor of so-called lay presidency of eucharistic celebrations. This latter point clearly corresponds to the insistence in AC Article XIV that those who officiate in the service of word and sacrament must be *rite vocatus* ("properly called"). And

[17] On the diaconate, see John Collins, *Diakonia: Reinterpreting the Ancient Sources* (Oxford: Oxford University Press, 1990). For an ecumenical discussion of this particular ministry, see *The Diaconate as Ecumenical Opportunity: The Hannover Report of the Anglican-Lutheran International Commission* (London, 1996).

[18] For a theological perspective on laity and the nature and purpose of their service, see Yves Congar, *Lay People in the Church: A Study for a Theology of Laity* (London: Geoffrey Chapman, 1959).

while Martin Luther stressed that all are like priests, bishops, and popes when it comes to *dignity* before God, there are obvious differences with regard to *functions and ministry*. We are all priests, but all of us are not presbyters, to allude to the New Testament terminology. Finally, it should also be noted that the so-called common priesthood is collective, in the sense that it primarily applies to God's people as a whole and only through the community does it apply to individuals.

Sacramentum Mundi— The Church and Its Mission in the World

The Church is not an isolated end in itself. Quite the contrary, being sent by Christ in the Holy Spirit, the Church participates in a dynamic mission that is realized in the Father's sending of the Son and the Son's sending of the Spirit. In the final analysis, the aim of this mission is "that the creation itself will be set free from its bondage to decay and will obtain the freedom of the glory of the children of God" (Rom 8:21). Moreover, it is God's plan to reconcile "all things in heaven and on earth" in Christ who is "the head of the body, the church" (Col 1:16ff.). Seen in this cosmic and eschatological perspective, the goal of the Church and its mission is not only that a number of souls shall be saved but that God's creation be redeemed. The framework and scope of the service of the Church cannot be confined to people's hearts or souls. What is at stake here is the drama of, or the dialectic between, creation and redemption. It is within such a framework that the Church is to be seen as "the priest of creation." However, when the world is considered to be largely irrelevant to the Church or when life in the Church is confused with some kind of escapism, there is something disastrously wrong, not so much with the world as with the Church. Admittedly, the Church is not *of* this world, but it is definitely *in* the world. And it is God who has placed it there.[19]

---

[19] On the relationship between Church and world in a general perspective, see Edward Schillebeeckx, *Church and World* (London: Sheed and Ward, 1971), and Gennadios Limouris, ed., *Church, Kingdom, World: The Church as Mystery and Prophetic Sign,* Faith and Order Paper No. 130 (Geneva: World Council of Churches, 1986). See further the Pastoral Constitution on the Church in the Modern World *(Gaudium et Spes)* from Vatican II and *Life in Christ: Morals, Communion and the Church* by the Second Anglican-Roman Catholic International Commission (1994). A good summary of more recent ecumenical debates on the relationship between ecclesiology and ethics can be found in Thomas F. Best and Martin Robra, eds., *Ecclesiology and Ethics: Ecumenical Ethical Engagement, Moral Formation and the Nature of the Church* (Geneva: World Council of Churches, 1997), which includes the

At the same time, however, the dead end of a purely "activist" ecclesiology must be avoided. For the Church is clearly more than the sum of its functions or external activities. Its identity is to be found just as much in what it *is,* in accordance with God's calling, as in what it *does* in its earthly shape or existence. It must be maintained that the Church necessarily "makes" mission, but mission does not necessarily "make" the Church as its sole constitutive feature. Furthermore, there is a certain truth to the slogan of the 1960s that "the world provides the church's agenda," as long as we realize that we are here talking about God's world and his creation. When such an awareness is missing, there is a danger that the service of the Church will disintegrate into a kind of secularized activism. The Church's sending to the world must be shaped by its proper identity and integrity; mission actually requires a firm sense of ecclesiological identity and consciousness, and approaches that might jeopardize this identity must be avoided. Any impression that there is some kind of competition or rivalry between service and identity in the Church's life requires correction. A reflection of this concern can be seen in a central message from the 1937 Oxford Conference on Life and Work: "Let the church be the church."

Where, then, does this lead us in more concrete terms? Let me start by indicating that there is much evidence that the difference between what may be labeled "secularized activism" and an "identity-based mission" becomes more visible in terms of the motivation and direction of our efforts than in view of the specific contents of our service. This corresponds to the fact that the aim of life in the Church is definitely not a sectarian escape from the world, but manifestation of the Church as the priest of creation. And surely, cooperation with "all persons of good will" is fully possible within such a framework.

It is helpful to recall the Church's service and appearance as an anticipatory sign of the kingdom of God in its fullness. According to the gospel, this kingdom is the place where the smallest are the greatest, the last come first, children are given priority, and "holy foolishness" is preferred to pompous earthly wisdom. This kingdom is radically different from the world and the societies we have developed, marked as they are by a lack of justice and massive inequality. A church that stands forth as an effective sign of this kingdom will, so to speak, by

---

vital WCC statements "Costly Unity" (1993), "Costly Commitment" (1994), and "Costly Obedience" (1996).

virtue of its mere existence emerge as an impetus for change and as a powerful counterculture. This church will be radically different from our broken world: it will be a place where things move toward becoming what was originally intended in the eyes of God the Creator and as that intention will finally be realized when his redemptive work in Christ has been fulfilled.[20] It should be further noted that the Church's function to be a sign of God's kingdom also means that its mission is placed in the framework of, and held together with, another crucial side of its identity, namely, its eschatological nature.

Another point where the positive interaction between the Church's nature or identity and its mission becomes clear is its character and calling as a *communio*-based fellowship in which love is an essential bond of unity (Col 3:14ff.) and in which we fulfill Christ's law by carrying one another's burdens (Gal 6:2). We have already seen that this community is established in the Eucharist and in its celebration as an *agape* meal in which sharing plays a key role. Today we live in a world in which such fellowship, on macro as well as micro levels, has become a most rare commodity. Instead of basing our choices on what serves our fellow human beings, there is an increased tendency to selfishly insist on rights while forgetting obligations. Such attitudes are totally incompatible with the Church's nature as the body of Christ and as community. To the extent that *communio*-based values and assets become concretely visible in the life of the Church, they will contribute to an unmasking and, it is to be hoped, also a corrective that societies lacking such virtues desperately need. It is precisely in this way that the Church can be seen as an effective sign of unity, sharing, and solidarity in a world marked by militant divisions and unrestricted selfishness.

Yet another example of "nature- or identity-based mission" can be found in the Church's existence as a community of hope, once more with a reference to its eschatological nature. On the one hand, there is today clearly a need for what the Finnish philosopher Georg Henrik von Wright has labeled "provocative pessimism" in order to expose and counteract the frantic but utterly futile "optimism of vanity" that makes many close their eyes to the immense challenges, particularly of environmental threats and the menace of a consumerist culture.[21] On the other hand, there appears to be a growing sense of meaningless-

---

[20] I have tried to develop this point further and with a particular view to church unity in "The Unity of the Church—What in the World Is It For?" *Pro Ecclesia* 5 (1996) 396ff.

[21] See Georg Henrik von Wright, *Myten om framsteget* (Stockholm: Almqvist 1993).

ness and lack of purpose among people—for some, arising from what the Czech author Milan Kundera has described as "the unbearable lightness of being"; for others, emerging as the inevitable consequence of desperate material deprivation. Seen in the light of such realities, it is vital to avoid "provocative pessimism" leading to widespread hopelessness. In facing this challenge, the Church's calling is to proclaim a living hope in Christ (see 1 Pet 3:15) and itself to be a community of hope, a community that carries a hope that is able to breed hope in the world, and thus is relevant to the whole of God's creation.

The description of the Church as *sacramentum mundi,* a sacrament in and for the world, provides a suitable perspective for summarizing what in the present chapter has been referred to as an identity-based mission. (1) This approach places the Church's mission and service firmly in an essential mark of the Church, that is, sacramentality and the individual sacraments. In the wake of this, it becomes evident that there is an interconnection between the Church's sacramental nature, our sacramental celebration, and our sacramental service in the world. (2) This concept also helps to avoid the counterproductive dichotomy between identity and mission that stems from passive escapism as well as secularized activism. Mission grows directly out of the Church's proper identity, its sacramental nature, while at the same time contributing to this identity. (3) Further, it reflects and affirms both the dynamic and the more ontological aspects of a sacramental approach; sacramentality is based primarily in the Church's *being* but still includes *doing.* (4) This kind of sacramentality must also be understood in a *sign* perspective or, more precisely, as an anticipatory sign of God's kingdom. To be sure, a total identification of *signum* and *res* (the sign and the reality it signifies) must be avoided. Yet it remains clear that the Church is to be an effective and most real representation of the kingdom. (5) The concept of *sacramentum mundi* provides in the Church's life an essential link between creation and redemption that makes it possible to integrate these two fundamental dimensions in a most fruitful manner. Actually, the Church itself becomes this linkage as a sacramental sign in and for the world.

We have thus far abstained from discussing questions concerning the relationship between service and evangelism, as well as between *diakonia* and *martyria.* Yet one brief observation should be made. It seems clear that a certain differentiation within the Church's mission is required. For even if social or political service in the world also must be seen in the perspective of the responsibility to witness to the gospel, there will on given occasions be a difference between such efforts and the preaching of the gospel to those who have never heard it. It would surely be disastrous if this vital part of being sent from Jerusalem to "the ends of the earth" (Acts 1:8) should be neglected.

Still, these concerns must be perceived basically as two sides of the same coin, or rather as integral parts of the one mission and vocation of the Church. For our commission and the final aim of all our efforts are one. It is meaningless to play varying aspects of this commission off against each other. In this way two ditches can be avoided. On the one side is the proclivity to tear mission and evangelism apart either by focusing solely on the traditional evangelistic task or by a biased overemphasizing of the social challenges. On the other side is an approach where everything the Church may do is understood as mission, overlooking that mission has a core and a *proprium*, that is, the communication of the gospel. Thus it becomes clear that the Church is *sacramentum mundi* in its service to the gospel in and for the world.[22]

The Nature of the Church—
One, Holy, Catholic, and Apostolic

When the Nicene Creed understands the Church as an object of faith by insisting on its *credo ecclesiam*, this can be seen as compatible with our description of the Church as the place or location of salvation. However, the Nicene Creed also offers a specific characterization of the Church we believe in by listing four *proprietates ecclesiae*, ecclesial "attributes" or "marks": unity, holiness, catholicity, and apostolicity. These attributes describe the essence of the true Church, and they serve as its key visible manifestations. This is a most appropriate foundation for our efforts to give a summarizing account of the Church's nature and its basic purpose.

Since we will return to the matter of the unity of the Church in the next chapter, our reflections here will be brief. It must be noted, however, that the Creed's listing of *unitas* among the essential attributes of the Church makes it clear that unity of necessity belongs to the Church's nature. This unity derives from the unity of the Triune God: since there is only one body, one God, one Lord, one Spirit, one faith, and one baptism (Eph 4:4ff.), there can only be one Church. It must, accordingly, be emphasized that basic unity is given in Christ; our task is never to cre-

---

[22] See Carl E. Braaten, *The Flaming Center: A Theology of the Christian Mission* (Philadelphia: Fortress Press, 1977).

ate unity, but rather to visualize it and make it manifest in and for the world. This takes place mainly through unity in faith and confession, through common celebration of the sacraments, and through unity in ministry, service, and mutual love. These are the primary bonds of unity within God's people. While a certain amount of diversity is both necessary and inevitable, these bonds continually direct us toward our calling to be a sign of visible unity in and for the world.

The holiness of the Church depends primarily on the fact that it belongs to God the Father, in the sense that he has called it into being through Christ and that it is the space of his continued action for the redemption of humankind in the Holy Spirit. Since everything that belongs to God is holy, it follows that the Church's holiness does not derive from our efforts or our longing for perfection, but from God's ultimate perfection and grace. Moreover, Christ is the supplier and champion of holiness, and the Holy Spirit strengthens us in our attempts to live a holy life. Further, penitence and the forgiveness it offers can be characterized, together with the cleansing effect of baptism and the anointment of confirmation as the sacrament of holiness. And our participation in the gift of holiness is celebrated in the Eucharist. All this implies that holiness can be and has been maintained within the Church even when it has failed its God-given purpose.

Yet our commitment and vocation to live holy lives remains an important sign of the Church's holiness. And despite the fact that our holiness as individuals and as God's people is a consequence of, and not a prerequisite for, the ecclesial mark of holiness, these concerns should never be torn apart. This happens, for example, when a kind of gospel-monism or antinomianism is allowed to lead to the forgetting or ignoring of God's law or his goodwill for all creation.

In light of this, it should be noted that the Church is the *communio sanctorum*, a fellowship gathered around the "holy things" or the means of grace and consisting of a people that has been made holy through these things.[23] This fellowship exists across time and space. Within the *communio sanctorum*, those who through the grace of God have gained a particular holiness, or the saints, play a key role. When seen "from above," the saints emerge as special recipients of God's effective grace and his ability to transform small and timid persons into brave

[23] Here a classical study by Werner Elert still calls for attention, *Eucharist and Church Fellowship in the First Four Centuries* (St. Louis: Concordia, 1966) German edition, 1954.

witnesses to the gospel. Seen "from below," the saints provide models for the faithful in their feeble attempts to live holy lives. This becomes particularly evident in light of the fact that sainthood and the veneration of the saints were often manifested in martyrdom. The classical biographies of the saints show that Christian holiness cannot be reduced to abstract ideas but must be concretely embodied in human lives and in the Church. In this way the saints reflect what true holiness is and serve as manifestations of the Church's holiness.[24]

Catholicity is the third essential mark of the Church.[25] It appears strange that the Norwegian and several other Protestant translations of the Creed have chosen to replace this concept with the far more vague term "common." What is at stake here is certainly not the Church's being ordinary or habitual in a folk churchlike or "folksy" manner, but rather its existence *kath' holou*, everywhere or in every place. This kind of catholicity is vertically grounded in the Church's communion with the Father through the Son in the Spirit. However, catholicity should also and must be manifested horizontally, witnessing to the Church as a sign of God's universal grace and corresponding with its fundamental unity. An early statement of this attribute—in addition to reflections in, for example, the letters of Ignatius of Antioch—can be found in Vincent of Lérin's so-called catholicity principle from the middle of the fifth century: *id teneamus quod ubique, quod semper, quod ab omnibus creditum est* (" we should maintain that which is believed everywhere, always, by all"—*Commonitory* 2, 6). Catholicity is both a quantitative and a qualitative entity, in the sense that it conveys a picture of the borders as well as the core of the faith of the one universal Church. Such catholicity, however, is not contrary to a certain amount of contextualization. One may even argue that true catholicity requires some kind of contextual embodiment in order to prevent it from ending up as an abstract principle. Nevertheless, a proper concern for catholicity shows that there are limits to contextuality, and those limits are transgressed when the universality of the Church and its faith are jeopardized.

Heresy is the blunt opposite of catholicity. While catholicity is focused on universality and the vast richness of the Church's faith, heresy

---

[24] A fascinating account of the historical roots and development of the Church's veneration of the saints can be found in Peter Brown, *The Cult of the Saints: Its Rise and Function in Latin Christianity* (Chicago: University of Chicago Press, 1981). See also Peter Brown, *Society and the Holy in Late Antiquity* (Berkeley: University of California Press, 1982).

[25] See Avery Dulles, *The Catholicity of the Church* (Oxford: Clarendon Press, 1987).

jeopardizes and violates universality by ignoring the integrity of this faith and by tearing the one body apart. A church that gives in to heresy immediately ceases to be a "pillar and bulwark of the truth" (1 Tim 3:15). In more concrete terms, heresy can be reductionist by downplaying or completely neglecting essential parts of the faith, or it can be maximalist by placing peripheral concerns at the center. But heresy always destroys the subtle balance of the "system" or "universe" of faith by neglecting the close interrelation between all its parts and by confusing the corpus of faith with the sum of more or less disconnected loci. Heresy necessarily becomes parochial and divisive. And since heresy is by nature schismatic, doctrinally as well as ecclesiologically, it also represents a most serious threat to the first Nicene mark of the Church, *unitas*.[26]

In opposing and fighting heresy, the fourth of the Nicene attributes, apostolicity, plays a key role. This mark serves as an effective reminder of, and a pointer toward, the Church's indispensable continuity both with the first apostles' witness to Christ and with the ensuing apostolic tradition. Simultaneously, it shows how this continuity can be expressed and safeguarded in the Church's life in concrete terms.[27] The signs of apostolicity are of crucial significance, especially the office of the ministry in general and the historic episcopal office in particular. I have already mentioned that this form of continuity was lost in several Lutheran churches, including those of Denmark, Norway, and Iceland, because of the ordination by Johannes Bugenhagen, who was not a bishop, of so-called superintendents in Copenhagen in 1537. However, this act should neither be theologized, nor should it be understood as a conscious break with the *successio apostolica*. What was at stake was rather the need of the evangelical congregations to secure some kind of episcopal oversight. And as this was denied them by the Roman Catholic Church, Bugenhagen's emergency solution seemed at the time to be the only possible measure.

Nevertheless, as a result of the loss of this sign of apostolic continuity, apostolicity often appears to have been reduced in some Lutheran

---

[26] For a more extensive discussion, see Ola Tjørhom: "'Heresy' and 'Unity in Faith': The Problem of Heresy in Ecumenical Perspective," *Studia Theologica* 48 (1994) 63ff. See also Karl Rahner, *On Heresy* (London: Burns and Oates, 1964); and Johannes Wirsching, *Kirche und Pseudokirche: Konturen der Häresie* (Göttingen: Vandenhoeck & Ruprecht, 1990).

[27] On apostolicity, see Carl Braaten, *The Apostolic Imperative: Nature and Aim of the Church's Mission* (Minneapolis: Augsburg Press, 1985) which stresses the interrelation between apostolicity and mission. See also *Apostolicity and Succession*, House of Bishops Occasional Paper (London: The Church of England, 1994).

circles to a rather abstract and invisible concern. Accordingly, it is now necessary to ask how this essential expression of apostolicity can be regained and revisualized today within the Reformation churches that have lost it without denying their apostolic past. This is one of the central intentions of the *Porvoo Common Statement* (1992) resulting from the dialogue between the Anglican churches in Great Britain and Ireland and the Lutheran churches in the Nordic and Baltic nations.

It can be helpful here to describe Porvoo's proposal for restoring continuity in the historic episcopate by the following brief theses:

1) Apostolicity should not be perceived solely as a link to the past, but rather as living continuity with the apostles' witness to Christ, and thus with Christ himself. Without such continuity, no true church can exist.

2) Since apostolic continuity is chiefly a continuity in faith and the confession of this faith, it becomes manifest when God's people confess the apostolic faith and thus emerges as a mark of the Church as a whole.

3) Being indispensable to the Church's life, apostolicity cannot be reduced to an abstract idea but requires visible manifestations. On the one hand, the signs and the "thing itself"—*signa* and *res*—should not be flatly identified. Apostolic continuity can also be kept up in periods when some of its signs have been lost. On the other hand, no church can afford to disregard one single feasible sign of this essential ecclesial mark, meaning that we should aim at embracing and including as many of these signs as possible.

4) The different signs of apostolicity should not be understood as being the private property of parochial churches. Apostolicity is expressed best in community, that is, when we share in each other's signs of apostolic continuity.

5) On this basis, the *Porvoo Common Statement* proposes that the churches that already possess the sign of historic continuity in the episcopal office are free to acknowledge the apostolicity of churches that have lost this particular sign, while these churches are free to regain it. Within this framework, fellowship and full interchangeability of ministries have been established between three types of churches: churches that cherish the historic episcopate as theologically essential; churches that have kept this sign without necessarily seeing it as ecclesiologically constitutive; and churches that have lost this form of *successio apostolica*. The approach advocated by the *Porvoo Common Statement* implies that the historic episcopate is understood neither as an ab-

solute juridical requirement nor as a mere optional extra in the Church's life, but as a gift to be received. However, it must be noted that all the Porvoo churches are episcopally ordered.[28]

In concluding this brief account of the Nicene *proprietates ecclesiae,* I would like to reiterate the following concerns. First, these attributes must be seen as clearly interrelated. This primarily means that the Church's holiness, expressing its belonging to God, and its apostolicity, emphasising its essential continuity with the apostolic witness to Christ, serve as the framework and foundation of its unity and catholicity. Second, even if the Church must fight continually to safeguard and express these marks in its life, they apply to the "real" or empirically existing church and not to some kind of heavenly or spiritual idea. Third, however, these attributes pertain first and foremost to the *una sancta* or the community of the Church, and only in consequence of this to individual churches. Accordingly, the ecclesiology of the Nicene Creed forcefully directs us toward commitment to church unity.

Conclusion: Visible Community—In and for the World

In summarizing this chapter on the nature and purpose of the Church, the concept of *communio* is particularly relevant and helpful. This concept is grounded in the vertical aspect of the Church in its *koinonia* with the Father through the Son in the Spirit; the Church can, then, be seen as a reflex and the location of our participation in the life of the Holy Trinity. However, this vertical dimension immediately and necessarily points to the horizontal or earthly aspects of the Church's life as both the priest of creation and a fellowship in which the restoration of true humanity has begun and will be completed. It is important to realize that these two fundamental concerns are closely interrelated: our vertical *communio* must be manifested horizontally, and our horizontal fellowship is based on and directed toward the vertical *koinonia.* As a matter of fact, these dimensions can never be torn apart from each other. In this way the "from above" and "from below" perspectives are also kept together. And once more, sacraments and sacramentality

---

[28] For a more comprehensive discussion of the *Porvoo Common Statement* in general and its approach to the apostolicity of the Church in particular, see my chapter "Apostolicity and Apostolic Succession in the *Porvoo Common Statement*—Necessary or a Mere 'Optional Extra' in the Church's Life?" in Ola Tjørhom, ed., *Apostolicity and Unity: Essays on the Porvoo Common Statement* (Grand Rapids: Eerdmans, 2002). In this book I present a more extensive account of what I have described as "the Porvoo model" for shared apostolicity.

provide an essential link, expressing both our participation in and with Christ and our truly human fellowship.[29]

I cannot here review in detail the *communio* concept and its vast and perhaps somewhat confusing richness. Yet I would like to underline certain key elements of the concept. (1) It should be noted that *communio* is more open to the great diversity or even affluence of the Church's life than other ecclesial images. The dead end of ecclesiological minimalism is avoided, and at the same time the immense ecumenical potential of this concept is laid bare. (2) The notion of *communio* demonstrates and actualizes the basic communal nature of life in Christ, while privatizing and individualizing attitudes are forcefully corrected. (3) The *communio* concept succeeds in holding together the central elements of Christian or ecclesial fellowship, that is, community in faith, community in sacramental celebration *(communio in sacris)*, community in ministry and mission, and community in mutual love and solidarity. (4) When the Church is seen as *communio,* its diachronic and synchronic dimensions as a fellowship that exists across time and space are reflected, and the essentially eschatological nature of the Church is also affirmed and expressed. (5) Since the sacramentally grounded and socially directed *communio* is basically visible, this concept also contributes to an affirmation of the fundamental visibility of the Church.[30]

When the visible nature of the Church is described, the main emphasis is often put on ecclesial and ministerial structures. Ironically, this is true both among strong proponents as well as fierce opponents of such structures. Now, it must surely be maintained that church structures in general and structures for authoritative teaching in particular contribute significantly to the Church's visibility and are not to be neglected. One may even argue that structures are essential to both the Church as such and to the unity in faith that is at the core of its life. Yet ecclesial visibility should not be identified with the structural aspect. Moreover, the ambiguity of structures must always be taken into

---

[29] Even if the point of departure here is the *"von oben"* dimension, it is at least a partly similar approach to that of Dietrich Bonhoeffer in his classic work *Sanctorum Communio: A Theological Study of the Sociology of the Church.* Dietrich Bonhoeffer Works, vol. 1 (Minneapolis: Fortress Press, 1998).

[30] A very important, more general presentation of the *communio* concept can be found in John D. Zizioulas, *Being as Communion: Studies in Personhood and the Church* (Crestwood, N.Y.: St. Vladimir's Seminary Press, 1993). See also Jean Tillard, *Église d'églises: L'ecclesiologie de communion* (Paris: Cerf, 1987), and the Second Anglican–Roman Catholic International Commission text *Church as Communion* (1991).

account, calling for a distinction between structures of the *una sancta* and structures that primarily aim at supporting and sustaining parochial institutions. In understanding the visibility of the Church, the constitutive means of grace offer a far more suitable point of departure. The key concern here is simply that the Church is just as empirically recognizable as the outward word and the visible sacraments that constitute it. At this point it should be reiterated that even if the Lutheran Reformers spoke of the Church as hidden *(verborgen)* in terms of its true members, they never understood it as essentially invisible.

Additionally, the crucial image of the Church as a body, the body of Christ, tends to become meaningless if it is associated with an invisible entity. Like every other body, the church body and its appropriate functioning as a body require visible "embodiment." In the final analysis, the most crucial concern is that the Church's visibility is directed toward its mission and service, partly in the sense that the fellowship it offers calls for concrete manifestation, and partly so that people will be able to *see* the Church and its unity and thus believe (see John 17:21).

Ecclesial visibility is not something radically different from the Church's spiritual nature, let alone something that on given occasions may even threaten this nature. On the contrary, we are talking about a visibility rooted in the factors that are at the core of the Church's spiritual life and mission. It must, therefore, be maintained that it is precisely as a spiritual reality that the Church is and must be basically visible. And as we shall see in subsequent chapters, this applies also to the spiritual unity of the Church as well as to the spiritual life unfolded within the Church.

Let me conclude this chapter by saying that at the core of my ecclesiological account there is a wish to open as many eyes as possible to the vast richness that is reflected in the life of the Church across time as well as space. Protestant minimalism has proven to be extremely counterproductive, not least as regards ecclesiology. Since the Church's richness is firmly rooted in God's many gifts to his people through Christ in the Holy Spirit, the often distressing fact that the Church is also a human institution that shares in the brokenness of human community may conceal our participation in the abundance that stems from the Triune God, but never destroy or exclude it. There is perhaps not so much that we *must* believe concerning the Church for the sake of our salvation. But there is certainly much that we both *can* and *should* believe, simply because it will be an immense enrichment to us.

Chapter 4

The Goal of Visible Unity—
Reaffirming Our Commitment

The goal of ecumenism has been described in many different ways. While the Roman Catholic Church before the Second Vatican Council was aiming, at least partly, at the return of "the separated brethren" to the Roman mother church, others were prepared to settle for an internal or spiritualized fellowship between individuals who had a common understanding of the gospel and Christian life. However, within the movement for church unity that started with the world conferences on Faith and Order and Life and Work and which was continued by the World Council of Churches after its formation in 1948, the ecumenical goal has traditionally been associated with some kind of *visible* unity. Allowing for a certain measure of variation, this goal has also been shared by several of the so-called Christian World Communions.

A classic expression, interpretation, and affirmation of the goal of visible unity can be found in the fundamental statement on church fellowship or the so-called unity formula of the third WCC Assembly in New Delhi in1961:

> We believe that the unity which is both God's will and his gift to his Church is being made visible as all in each place who are baptized into Jesus Christ and confess him as Lord and Saviour are brought by the Holy Spirit into one fully committed fellowship, holding the one apostolic faith, preaching the one Gospel, breaking the one bread, joining in common prayer, and having a corporate life reaching out in witness and service to all and who at the same time are united with the whole Christian fellowship in all places and all ages in such wise that ministry and

members are accepted by all, and that all can act and speak together as occasion requires for the tasks to which God calls his people.[1]

In several later texts the New Delhi unity formula has been further developed, always with an emphasis on the goal of visible unity. An example of this can be found in the Catholic- Lutheran dialogue document *Facing Unity:*

> The unity of the church given in Christ and rooted in the Triune God is realized in our unity in the proclaimed word, the sacraments and the ministry instituted by God and conferred through ordination. It is lived both in the unity of the faith to which we jointly witness, and which together we confess and teach, and in the unity of hope and love which leads us to unite in fully committed fellowship. Unity needs a visible outward form which is able to encompass the element of inner differentiation and spiritual diversity as well as the element of historical change and development. This is the unity of a fellowship which covers all times and places and is summoned to witness and serve the world.[2]

Such statements clearly indicate that within the ecumenical movement there has been a strong commitment to the goal of visible unity. What is at stake here is a unity in faith and the confession of this faith, a unity in the sacraments and in sacramental celebration, and a unity in ministry, mission, and love. Moreover, there has been a growing awareness that such unity calls for structural expressions that make it concretely visible. Today, however, there is much evidence that we are witnessing a shift here: instead of visible structured unity, the main emphasis seems to be put increasingly on a static "diversity" which is based on a typically "postmodern" worshiping of limitless plurality and which allows the churches to maintain their denominational or even parochial identities and so to "remain as they are." In my view this trend has become particularly strong within German and continental European liberal-pietistic Protestantism.[3]

---

[1] See the whole New Delhi statement on church unity in W. A Visser't Hooft, ed., *The New Delhi Report: The Third Assembly of the World Council of Churches, 1961* (London: SCM Press, 1962) 116–125.

[2] See the Roman Catholic/Lutheran Joint Commission, *Facing Unity: Models, Forms and Phases of Catholic-Lutheran Church Fellowship* (Geneva: Lutheran World Federation, 1985) §3. Actually, the New Delhi formula is quoted in the next paragraph of *Facing Unity,* and *Facing Unity* §4 is quoted in §26 of the *Porvoo Common Statement* from the dialogue between the British and Irish Anglican Churches and the Nordic and Baltic Lutheran Churches.

[3] I have discussed the ecumenical profile of what I label "German Continental Protestantism" in "The Goal of Visible Unity—Reaffirming Our Commitment," *The Ecumenical*

The aim of what follows is not to present an outline of a complete ecumenical theology. Nor shall I repeat the heated debates of the 1970s and 1980s on so-called models of unity. I strongly doubt that church fellowship can appropriately be accounted for by using more or less abstract "models." It is significant that several recent dialogue texts, for example, the *Porvoo Common Statement* of 1992 and *Called to Common Mission* of 1999, both from Anglican-Lutheran dialogues, clearly transcend the traditional "models" approach. In any case, the key aim at present is to discuss further the rather discouraging development pointed to in the last paragraph. I also hope to contribute to a reaffirmation of the goal of visible unity. Such a reaffirmation will be in keeping not only with the view of the World Council of Churches and its predecessor bodies but also with the evangelical catholic movement particularly as expressed in "the Great Tradition of the Church."

More Plurality and Less Visibility

The evident decline in commitment to the goal of visible unity does not depend solely on theology and theological shifts. Philosophical and more generally popular cultural currents also play a crucial role. While modernity largely was marked by a vision of unity and a parallel concept of unifying or common truths, an almost laissez fairelike pluralism seems to be the preferred late modern or postmodern solution. Within the churches, this change has often been welcomed as a positive opportunity, since it leaves a certain space for the religious dimension. However, this space does not provide for the "objective" truth claims of religion, but merely for a kind of curiosity over against a vast variety of religious experiences that seem to be viewed on the same level as experiences offered by the media, the entertainment

---

Review 54, no. 1–2 (2002) 162ff. This paper is the foundation of my reflections in the present chapter. Among other things, I stress that German continental Protestantism is rooted in contemporary liberal-pietism, that it dominates the Protestant arena on the European continental scene, particularly within the Evangelical Church in Germany, and that it has the *Leuenberg Concord* between Reformed, United, and Lutheran churches in Europe from 1973 as its main ecumenical expression. On the basis partly of the observation that we are here confronted with a consequence of the postmodern adoration of plurality and partly of the fact that Leuenberg has a North American equivalent, namely, *A Formula of Agreement Between the Evangelical Lutheran Church in America, the Presbyterian Church (USA), the Reformed Church in America, and the United Church of Christ* of 1997 (even being presented as an expression of "full communion"), it can be stated that this position is also of relevance within the American context.

industry, and other populist cultural agents. This claimed postmodern openness to religion may easily turn out to be a Pyrrhic victory for the churches. Ecumenically speaking, its repercussions are less than gratifying, especially since it leaves room for an endless row of parochial or isolated "identities." It should, of course, be added that we are also facing expressions of heavily oppressive uniformism today, particularly in the form of racism and militant intolerance. Such attitudes, however, can effectively be countered only by a firm insistence on truth and justice and not by vague and uncommitted pluralism.

Our main concern in this connection, however, is not postmodern pluralism, but rather its theological parallels. Such attitudes clearly play an increasingly central role today, as can be traced even in developments within the World Council of Churches. This can be seen by the fact that in comparison with the above quoted unity formula from the New Delhi Assembly, deliberations on this topic at the Harare Assembly in 1998 were far more ambiguous. The Assembly Message from Harare, to be sure, contains references to the goal of visible unity, but at the same time there appears to be an increasing focus on the idea of a "Forum of Christian Churches and Ecumenical Organisations" that hardly equals the New Delhi vision of an organic communion between truly united local churches within "one fully committed fellowship." Recently renewed affirmations of the so-called Toronto Statement of 1950 and its idea—in practice understandable but theologically rather peculiar—that the World Council should be marked by an "ecclesiological neutrality" point in the same direction.[4]

However, European continental Protestantism seems clearly to be the most important agent of theological pluralism today. The ideal of a basically common faith has been sacrificed in order to allow for the incorporation and accommodation of nearly anything people may choose to believe. Moreover, the unifying function of the liturgy is being jeopardized by radical contextualization and constant reinvention. Some even hold that rites or rituals can only be meaningful when

---

[4] Concerning the deliberations on church unity in Harare, see Diane Kessler, ed., *Together on the Way: Official Report of the Eighth Assembly of the World Council of Churches* (Geneva: WCC Publications, 1999), especially "Being Together Under the Cross in Africa: The Assembly Message," pp. 1–5, and the report of the WCC general secretary Dr. Konrad Raiser to the Assembly on December 4, 1998, in which the idea of "forum" played a key role. The title of the Toronto statement is "The Church, the Churches, and the World Council of Churches: The Ecclesiological Significance of the World Council of Churches," received by the WCC Central Committee in Toronto in 1950.

they are designed to meet the private needs of individuals, ignoring their corporate nature. Within many Protestant churches, there is also a strong emphasis on parochial identities of a sub-theological nature. In my opinion, the *Leuenberg Concord* from the dialogue between Lutheran, Reformed, and United Churches on the European continent (1973) can be seen as an early example of this pluralist ecumenical approach. The central concern of this agreement appears to be that church unity be expressed through "mutual recognition" between churches that remain different. The text of the *Leuenberg Concord* goes so far as to recommend a mutual recognition of the ordained ministries of the signatory churches, while being virtually silent on how these ministries should be understood theologically.[5] In a recent statement on ecumenism by the Evangelical Church in Germany (EKD), this approach is driven almost *in absurdum* by repeatedly confusing the goal of visible unity with something that is called *ein geordnetes Miteinander bekenntnisverschiedener Kirchen,* an ordered togetherness of churches that have different confessions.[6] In the following some of the characteristic theological features and implications of this Protestant pluralist ecumenism will be identified.[7]

1) The point of departure is a general ecclesiological deficit by which the Church is understood as essentially invisible. This is based on a confusion of the Lutheran Reformers' view that the "real church," the *ecclesia proprie dicta,* is to be understood as hidden *(verborgen)* in regard to its true members, with an insistence that the Church as such is invisible. As a consequence of this misinterpretation, the Church tends to emerge as a kind of *societas platonica,* or as a mere "idea" that has no "body." At best, this church is capable of serving as a purely practical framework for religious sentiments; at worst, it becomes a direct impediment to authentic religion. When the Church is described as fundamentally invisible, there will be no room for the concept of visible church unity, let alone for a perception of visibility that includes concrete ecclesial structures.

---

[5] The text of the *Leuenberg Concord* and a certain amount of discussion of its contents can be found in William G. Rusch and Daniel F. Martensen, eds., *The Leuenberg Agreement and Lutheran-Reformed Relationships: Evaluation by North American and European Theologians* (Minneapolis: Augsburg Press, 1989).

[6] See the statement of the Evangelical Church in Germany, *Kirchengemeinschaft nach evangelischem Verständnis* (September 29, 2001) in *Texte der EKD*, Nr. 69, 2001.

[7] See also my critical assessment of post-Reformation Protestantism in Chapter 1 above, pp. 5–10.

2) This ecclesiological deficit corresponds to an epistemological peculiarity by which theology in general and ecclesiology in particular are turned into a series of abstract principles or "ideas" that are not properly embedded either in the reality of the Church or in human life. The most obvious example of this is an understanding of the doctrine of justification in which this doctrine is torn apart not only from its ecclesiological-sacramental framework but also from its christological-trinitarian basis. One occasionally gets the impression that it is "the doctrine of justification" that saves, and not Christ. This "idealistic" obsession is at least partly grounded in Hegel's thought as filtered through Schleiermacher's description of religion as *Gefühl* ("feeling"). Thus a perhaps somewhat outdated Hegel appears to be alive and kicking among German or continental European Protestants. The same seems to be the case with Kant's denial of the ontological aspects of theology and of its capacity to say something about the world and being as it really is. There is a certain tendency in these circles to treat yesterday's news as if they came down *senkrecht von oben* ("directly from heaven").

3) Further, ecumenical theology is also often pursued within German Protestantism on the basis of abstract principles or ideas. This takes shape in the form of a steadfast belief that unity can be achieved through presumedly sophisticated methodological acrobatics frequently labeled "ecumenical methodology." According to this approach, we are only supposed to agree on foundational "ideas," an enterprise that will allow us to keep our densely parochial faiths and our even more parochial practices unchanged and unchallenged. A good example of this attitude can be found in the insistence that we should reach concord on an abstract *Grund* ("foundation"), while continuing to present this *Grund* in radically differing or even directly contrary *Gestalten* ("shapes"). Thus one seems to presume that there is such a thing as a *Grund* without a *Gestalt*, which is seriously to be doubted.

4) Within continental Protestantism, the protection of particular or even parochial identities seems to be a strong priority. As already indicated, these identities often appear to be of a sub-theological kind, in the sense that they depend just as much on national, popular, or densely denominational factors as on proper theology. European Evangelical Protestants have been concerned to develop ecumenical concepts that allow for a combination of particular identities with an ecumenical obligation. The idea of "mutual recognition" between the churches plays a crucial role here. A form of recognition or acknowledgment can be a vital step toward unity, but it should not be confused

with the ecumenical goal itself, particularly not when it is applied as a measure that allows the churches to "remain as they are." This kind of approach seems at least to be a possible consequence of the *Leuenberg Concord*. Another, perhaps even more striking, example of this can be found in the *Reuilly Common Statement* from the dialogue between the Anglican churches in Great Britain and Ireland and the French Lutheran and Reformed churches (1997). In this text the Protestant dialogue partner maintains that according to an evangelical perception, "mutual recognition" includes both "full communion" and "full interchangeability of ministries."[8] Such views seem to associate ecumenism more with joint signing of diplomatic treaties than with common life in Christ.

5) As a consequence of this, there is a tendency within European Evangelical Protestantism to confuse the steps toward unity with the goal of unity. This is reflected in the radically divergent interpretations of the *Meissen Common Statement* from the dialogue between the Church of England and the Evangelical Church in Germany (1988). While the Anglican partner maintains that this agreement must be seen as a step on the way toward unity, German Protestants claim that the achieved "mutual recognition" is all that is needed for unity, a position actually taken against the explicit words of the *Meissen Common Statement* itself. A similar attitude can, in my opinion, be uncovered in a typical Protestant approach to the question of intercommunion. In an eagerness to bring about forms of a so-called eucharistic hospitality, many Protestants seem to understand the Eucharist more as a means to realize unity than as an expression of unity. Considerable pressure in this regard has been put on the Roman Catholic Church especially, even though something is being asked for that Protestants should know Catholics cannot give. Obviously this is done without there being anything close to a sharing of a common eucharistic faith.

These factors together point toward a static understanding of ecclesial diversity and a similarly static concept of unity in which there is literally no room for change or for continued growth in unity. In the vocabulary of European Evangelical Protestants, this understanding is described as an "ecumenism of contradictions" *(Ökumene in Gegensätzen)*.[9] Moreover, parochial identities are often emphasized more

---

[8] See *Called to Witness and Service: The Reuilly Common Statement with Essays on Church, Eucharist and Ministry* (London: Church House Publishing, 1999).The quotation is taken from §27 of the *Reuilly Common Statement*.

[9] See here Eric Geldbach, *"Ökumene in Gegensätzen: Mit der Memorandum 'Reformatorische Kirchen und ökumenische Bewegung' in deutscher und englischer Sprache"* (Göttingen:

strongly than the commitment to unity. In this way all the impulses and gifts that are presented to us by Christians from other traditions are largely disregarded, and the fact that Christian identity must always be defined with a view to the Church of Christ as a whole is ignored. In such a framework, René Beaupère's vital insistence that "the reconciled church lies beyond all existing ecclesial realities" appears to be totally forgotten.[10] This seems to indicate that German Protestants have exchanged the goal of visible unity for a basically friendly but still highly static and largely invisible "co-existence" in which the different churches are allowed to remain as they are. Such an invisible fellowship can hardly fulfill its purpose as an effective sign of, and witness to, unity in a divided world.

I would like to stress that the Protestant coupling of static diversity and an understanding of church fellowship as largely invisible with a traditional liberal-pietistic reductionist approach to the Church's faith has significant implications for the ecumenical enterprise as a whole. This becomes particularly evident when unity in the rich deposit of the faith of the Church is abandoned for a rather loose adherence to a minimalist least common doctrinal denominator. Within such a framework, the fundamental conviction that ecumenism is supposed to make us richer and not poorer tends to be forgotten. At the same time, we fall significantly short of the common life in Christ that is finally at stake.

"Reconciled Diversity" as "Reconciled Denominationalism"?

The intense debates of the 1970s and 1980s on the so-called "models of unity" turned out to be, in my view, of somewhat limited relevance.[11] On the one hand, these debates may have contributed to a cer-

---

Vandenhoeck & Ruprecht, 1987). An even more striking example of what I have characterized as a static ecumenical concept and a static perception of diversity can be found in Eilert Herms, *"Einheit der Christen in der Gemeinschaft der Kirchen: Die ökumenische Bewegung der römischen Kirche im Lichte der reformatorischen Theologie. Antwort auf den Rahner-Plan"* (Göttingen: Vandenhoeck & Ruprecht, 1984).

[10] See René Beaupère, "What Sort of Unity? The Decree of Ecumenism Ten Years Later—A Roman Catholic View," in *What Kind of Unity?* Faith and Order Paper No. 69 (Geneva: World Council of Churches, 1974) 32ff., at 38.

[11] Concerning the debate regarding "models" in general, see Günther Gassmann and Harding Meyer, *The Unity of the Church: Requirements and Structures,* Lutheran World Federation Report No. 15 (Geneva: Lutheran World Federation, 1983). Harding Meyer has played a most central and constructive role in the debates on the goal of unity. See

tain convergence on the ecumenical goal, and thus to a common sense of direction and purpose within the ecumenical movement. On the other hand, most of these concepts seem to be overly denomination-ally conditioned. This indicates that insights from several models must be combined in our efforts to describe church fellowship. We have also seen that many recent dialogue statements clearly transcend the tradi-tional models. Moreover, any belief that the pursuit of community can be founded on more or less abstract models requires correction. There is a need for an approach that is able to reflect the reality of the Church or of the churches in a more comprehensive and palpable way, for in-stance, along the lines of the ecclesiology of *communio.*

Here we wish to spend some time on one much discussed ecu-menical model, namely, unity in reconciled diversity. This model has frequently been characterized as *the* Lutheran model of unity.[12] When the concept in question was launched, roughly three decades ago, its main intention was to offer an approach that would grant some space for confessional diversity within ecumenical endeavors. Yet reconciled diversity was originally applied not as a concession to isolated or parochial denominational identities, but rather as a natural reflection of the many gifts that churches were committed to share with each other within the framework of communion. Additionally, there was a notable focus on the element of reconciliation which pointed toward the basic visibility of church fellowship. A long and heated debate con-cerning the relation between "reconciled diversity" and "conciliar fel-lowship," the then preferred model of the World Council of Churches, was concluded with a widely shared assertion that the two models were largely compatible. Let me add here that the father of the model of reconciliation, Harding Meyer, obviously sees the "organic" unity plan of the Catholic-Lutheran dialogue text *Facing Unity* (1985) as fully congruent with the notion of reconciled diversity.[13] Generally speaking,

---

in this connection his *That All May Be One: Perceptions and Models of Ecumenicity,* trans. William G. Rusch (Grand Rapids: Eerdmans, 1999). Among several other important con-tributions to this crucial question, see especially Yves Congar, *Diversity and Communion* (London: SCM Press, 1984).

[12] Even if "reconciled diversity" has never officially been declared the ecumenical model of the Lutheran World Federation, statements from the LWF General Assemblies in Dar-es-Salaam in 1977 and Budapest in 1984 point in this direction.

[13] As Lutheran drafter and advisor in the dialogue commission, Harding Meyer wrote significant parts of *Facing Unity.* Let me here also mention that the text includes a most helpful description of the different models of unity.

Facing Unity is a most valuable and helpful ecumenical statement, especially when it comes to its crucial concern for converting achieved consensus into concrete fellowship. Still, this statement has become the text that European Protestants really "love to hate."

During the last few decades, however, there have been significant shifts in the interpretation and application of reconciled diversity. This also seems to have been Harding Meyer's view when in 1988 he described this model as "a concept in crisis," taking exception to certain recent interpretations of the model.[14] What has happened is that reconciled diversity has been coopted by certain elements within European Evangelical or Protestant ecumenism and has been reshaped in order to meet particular needs and purposes. Today this reshaped model seems to rule the waves within the Leuenberg fellowship, but in a clearly minimalist version.[15] More concretely, the model of reconciliation has been adjusted in accordance with the principles of Protestant ecumenism as they have been listed above, with the result that reconciled diversity has been converted into a static, invisible, and rather idealistic concept that could be called "reconciled denominationalism." Reconciliation is reduced to the level of an abstract idea along the line of "an ordered togetherness of churches with different confessions," as the Evangelical Church in Germany has described the ecumenical goal.

This understanding of reconciled diversity often goes together with a narrow and minimalist interpretation of the basic requirements of unity as expressed in the *satis est* of AC Article VII. In some cases this article is even turned upside down, being interpreted as calling for an almost totalitarian uniformity in regard to order, while allowing for limitless diversity concerning the Church's faith and confession. Some problems that are attached to this Protestant interpretation of AC Article VII in general and the differentiation between *satis est* and *nec necesse* in particular have already been noted above in our first chapter. Let me here only repeat that the main difficulty is that the *satis/nec necesse* principle is falsely confused with rigid minimalism, and then, in this minimalist shape, is turned into a fundamental theological and ecclesiological principle that widely exceeds its original, more practi-

---

[14] See Harding Meyer, "'Unity in Diversity'—A Concept in Crisis: Lutheran Reflections," *One in Christ* 24 (1988) 128ff. Originally this paper was presented at a meeting of the Anglican Consultative Council.

[15] See the main theme and emphasis of the last assembly of the Leuenberg fellowship in Belfast, June 2001.

cal intention, which was to find a *modus vivendi* with regard to the Roman Catholic Church of the sixteenth century.

The central question today is whether the model of reconciliation can be rescued. Some seem to believe that it can; I must confess that I have serious doubts. This depends partly on the fact that reconciled diversity shares in the general ambiguity of the ecumenical models, in that they all require substantial supplementation in order to function constructively. Even more crucially, however, there is much evidence that the Protestant "Babylonian captivity" of the original understanding of reconciled diversity has simply lasted too long. For just as a leopard will have a hard time changing its spots, it becomes increasingly difficult to see how reconciled diversity can dissociate itself from static pluralism. One may argue that this is a result chiefly of a history of misuse. Yet in a situation where the crucial challenge is to reaffirm a commitment to the goal of *visible* unity over against the postmodern adoration of pluralism, it becomes increasingly clear that the model of reconciliation is marked by significant and inherent shortcomings. In such a situation, it is crucial to recognize that all factors that threaten to obscure or jeopardize unity constitute the ultimate borderline of beneficial or legitimate diversity. Accordingly, there seems to be ample reason to start looking for alternative concepts that may serve the goal of visible structured unity in a better way.

Basic Requirements and Steps toward Church Unity

Ecumenical models or concepts are not meaningful per se or in an isolated sense, but only when they are filled with specific theological content. Thus our search for a new or alternative concept of unity must start with an effort to identify the theological foundation of communion.[16] This foundation must always be defined not within a vacuum of abstraction but with a view to the practical realization of unity. Seen against this background, three fundamental questions emerge as crucial: First, what is the nature of ecumenical consensus? Second, what are the basic theological criteria or requirements of church fellowship?

---

[16] On the nature of theological or ecumenical consensus in a general perspective, see among other works, Joseph A. Burgess, ed., *In Search of Christian Unity: Basic Consensus/Basic Difference* (Minneapolis: Fortress Press, 1991), and André Birmele and Harding Meyer, eds., *Grundkonsens—Grunddifferenz: Studie des Strassburger Instituts für ökumenische Forschung. Ergebnisse und Dokumente* (Frankfurt am Main: Otto Lembeck; Paderborn: Bonifatius-Verlag, 1992).

And third, how can such a fellowship be accomplished in concrete terms? These questions are both wide-ranging and complicated and cannot be reviewed in detail here. We shall restrict ourselves to some brief remarks and observations.

When it comes to an understanding of the nature of consensus, there is at present much evidence that the traditional "ecumenism of consensus" is approaching its limits. This is manifested by the fact that there is a marked tendency within most ecumenical dialogues to re-open, without breaking new ground, questions that have been discussed in previous talks. Thus the dialogues increasingly resemble an endless piling up of abstract consensus none of which is converted into living fellowship. A similar lack of dynamics can be uncovered in the crucial matter of reception. To the extent that dialogue results are received at all, the challenge of reception is often leveled down to the question of whether a text should be formally signed and adopted as a possible interpretation of the faith, while concrete implementation of the signed statements in the lives of the churches is largely neglected.

Moreover, there is a proclivity to value ecumenical agreements only up to the point where they require specific changes in the churches. A discouraging example of this attitude can be found in the Church of Norway. Just after signing the *Porvoo Common Statement*, which makes it absolutely clear that "bishops ordain," the bishops' conference voted to continue the practice of letting cathedral deans preside at ordinations. Generally, we seem to have turned the approach to consensus of the New Testament and the ancient Church more or less upside down. The early Church insisted on unity in the christological-trinitarian core of faith, while providing space for a rich diversity in other areas. Today, however, churches often possess a basic unity on the core, but still press for uniformity on a number of peripheral and denominationally conditioned issues.

The current crisis in doctrinal ecumenism is based mainly on the fact that we are caught in a deadlock between confessionalist maximalism and indifferent minimalism. However, neither of these approaches represents an appropriate answer today. On the one hand, there is a need to distinguish between the center and the periphery within the universe of faith; there are examples that a confusion of these two dimensions may lead to heresy. On the other hand, efforts to identify a neat and tiny doctrinal common denominator also emerge as a dead end. Such attempts may cut us off from the richness, through time and space, of the Church's faith. Let me add that not only confessionalist maximalism but also reductionist minimalism can be categorical to the point of authoritarianism. It must once more be stressed that church fellowship is supposed to lead us into a common life, and it cannot be reduced to an alliance between people who merely have the same theological opinions.

It may well be that the notion of "differentiated consensus" offers the best answer to the question of the nature of ecumenical consensus.[17] In specifying the implications of this approach, five concerns play a key role: (1) A differentiated consensus embraces both a basic agreement and remaining differences. (2) This kind of consensus presupposes a differentiation between church-dividing and non-dividing issues, along the lines of the Roman Catholic notion of a "hierarchy of truths" *(hierarchia veritatum)*, the Orthodox emphasis on an "economy" *(oikonomia)* of faith, and the Lutheran distinction between what is sufficient and what is not necessary in order to realize communion. (3) However, the present differentiation should not be perceived primarily as a perspective on the deposit of faith as a whole, which tends toward a reductionist distinction between center and periphery. It must rather be seen as an approach to be applied to each "article" or item of faith. (4) The building of consensus and its reception should be understood as a dialectic between "recognition" and "enrichment" in which we recognize our faith or the Church's faith through the ages in the witness of our fellow Christians and at the same time are deeply enriched by the incorporation of new impulses. (5) Ecumenical consensus is definitely not only a question of doctrinal agreement; it also aims at a common life that includes unity in the celebration of the sacraments, in prayer, in structures of decision, and in a common mission in and for the world.

These reflections on the nature of theological consensus help us to identify the basic requirements of communion. The conviction that what constitutes the Church also constitutes church fellowship can be seen as our point of departure. It has already been asserted that this point of departure should not be interpreted in a minimalist or reductionist way. The subsequent requirements or criteria should also not be perceived as a set of juridical presuppositions for community, but rather as expressions

---

[17] Concerning the idea of a "differentiated consensus," see Harald Wagner, ed., *Einheit—aber wie? Zur Tragfähigkeit der ökumenischen Formel vom "differenzierten Konsens"* (Freiburg: Herder, 2000). Since Harding Meyer also played a highly crucial role in introducing this notion, I refer particularly to his essay in this volume, "Die Prägung einer Formel: Ursprung und Intention," 36ff.

and manifestations of unity that identify areas in which we are particularly committed to share our gifts with others. Furthermore, the fundamental criteria for unity are not merely something we must agree on in an abstract sense but something that is to be lived out in community. The following five factors play a particularly crucial role in efforts to account for the theological foundation of church fellowship:

1) Since faith is essential to Christian life, a fundamental unity in faith and the confession of this faith is an indispensable requirement for unity. This unity must be anchored primarily, if not exclusively, in the Word of God as contained in Holy Scripture and witnessed to by the Church. A basic expression of such unity is already available in the Nicene Creed. The central rule will be to "speak the truth in love" (Eph 4:14).

2) Christian life is essentially sacramental, initiated in baptism and nourished and fulfilled in the Eucharist. Other sacramental signs and acts that express and sustain our being in Christ also play a vital role. Thus there can be no communion without unity in sacramental life. This unity must include joint celebration of the sacraments as well as a mutual recognition of sacramental validity.

3) Since God's people is a structured people that includes shepherds and leaders, communion also entails unity in the various forms of the Church's ordained ministry. This unity will include full interchangeability of ministries and concelebration of the Eucharist. It also requires forms of common ordinations. Further, in its capacity as a special sign of unity and continuity, the office of the bishop is of particular significance here.

4) The goal of the Church is not only that a number of souls shall be saved but that God's creation be redeemed. The Church stands forth as the priest of creation and the first fruit of a reunited humankind. Accordingly, the unity we long for must embrace mission and service, always perceiving unity as being in and for the world.

5) Holy Scripture describes love as the bond that binds everything together "in perfect harmony" (Col 3:14). Thus the Church must be seen as a community of mutual love, which functions as an essential expression of unity. This love includes concrete solidarity and sharing, for when we "bear one another's burdens," we fulfill the law of Christ (Gal 6:2). Mutual love actually provides the framework for all other criteria for unity.

Neither the criterion concept as such nor individual criteria should be interpreted in a minimalist or reductionist way. What is at stake is the richness of the Church's experience and witness across time and space. Ecumenical commitment involves being constantly challenged by all the gifts that our sister churches are able to share with us—an immense source of mutual enrichment. Once again it becomes clear that ecumenism is not supposed to make us poorer but richer.

Finally, the practical realization of unity takes place through steps and stages that are connected with the aforementioned criteria. This points toward a so-called processual approach in which community is brought about through a dynamic growth in fellowship. An "all or nothing" solution, claiming that we either have full communion or no communion at all, emerges as counterproductive. The identification of concrete steps toward unity depends, among other things, on the ecumenical partners themselves. These steps will normally include an initial mutual recognition that the involved churches belong to the Church of Jesus Christ, a common worship life and celebration of the sacraments, and the development of joint structures for authoritative decisions and mission.[18]

We have, however, seen that it is essential to prevent preliminary steps toward unity from being muddled up with the ecumenical goal. Furthermore, a process understanding of the realization of church fellowship and the rejection of an "all or nothing" approach should not be confused with a subtle "grading" of communion. There is basically communion and non-communion, and then there are steps toward unity as well as a continual, eschatologically directed growth in unity. But there is no such thing as "half-full," or for that matter "half-empty," communion. I find it increasingly difficult to characterize bilateral fellowships or fellowships between limited numbers of partners as "full communion." This concept should probably be reserved for the ultimate unity of all God's people when Christ returns to fulfill his work.

Why Visible Unity and What Kind of Diversity? A Pneumatological Approach

At the core of most, perhaps even all, efforts to outline a workable ecumenical concept or model, there is a wish to contribute to a well-balanced perception of the dialectic between unity and diversity. This

[18] Both the statement of the Roman Catholic/Lutheran Joint Commission on *Ways to Community* (Geneva: Lutheran World Federation, 1981) and the already mentioned text *Facing Unity* from the same dialogue contain lists of steps toward unity.

dilemma played a key role in the life of the early church in its efforts to distinguish viable diversity from schismatic heresy.[19] In the seventeenth century the problem was formulated in a sharp and perceptive manner by Blaise Pascal when he suggested that "diversity without unity leads to confusion, while unity without diversity is tyranny."[20] Furthermore, we encounter the same dilemma in an acute form today, torn between postmodern pluralism and the goal of visible unity. In the following reflections, we shall endeavor to indicate how these two concerns can be understood and kept together generally, as well as with a particular view to the present ecumenical situation.

Let us start with ecclesial diversity and its ecumenical significance. Diversity belongs intrinsically to the life of the Church, reflecting the vast richness of this life. There is no true church fellowship without a significant degree of diversity, in a contextual as well as a more specific theological sense. Unity is never to be confused with total uniformity: "Unity in Christ does not exist despite and in opposition to diversity, but is given *with and in diversity*."[21] This approach to ecclesial diversity suggests that we should relate to such diversity as gifts that are offered by God through our Christian sisters and brothers. It also suggests that the Church may with humility and generosity offer a model or pattern of how diversity should be handled in a world that really struggles with this challenge. Yet diversity in the life of the Church should not be confused either with general liberalism and so-called low thresholds or with a practically and tactically motivated concession to theological pluralism. True ecclesial diversity must rather be seen as a specific theological or pneumatological entity that is firmly grounded in God's many and abundant gifts to the Church through Christ in the Holy Spirit.

This implies, on the one hand, that no church can afford to neglect or refuse a single one of God's gracious gifts. Moreover, the Spirit does not only "tolerate" a certain amount of ecclesial diversity but actively generates and sustains such diversity. Within this framework, it may

---

[19] On the struggle of the first Christians to hold together unity and diversity, see James D. G. Dunn, *Unity and Diversity in the New Testament: An Inquiry into the Character of Earliest Christianity* (Philadelphia: Westminster Press; London: SCM Press, 1977). On heresy and unity more generally, see Ola Tjørhom, "'Heresy' and 'Unity in Faith': The Problem of Heresy in Ecumenical Perspective," *Studia Theologica* 48 (1994) 63ff.

[20] "La multitude qui ne se réduit point à l'unité est confusion; l'unité qui ne dépend pas de la multitude est tyrannie." *Pensées;* Frag. LM 848/Br. 871.

[21] *Ways to Community,* §34.

even be argued that a uniformist oppression of diversity is not only a loss but a sin. On the other hand, what is at stake is not a general post-modern pluralism in which all things are equally acceptable, but rather the rich diversity of God's gifts given in the Holy Spirit. And the Spirit does not only generate diversity but also holds and binds our diversities together within the one body of the Church, as explained in a most forceful way by St. Paul in 1 Corinthians 12.

Subsequent to this, it must be clearly stated that diversity has its limits. These limits are drawn by God's goodwill for his creation, over against persistence in heresy and everything that puts unity in Christ in jeopardy. Seen in this perspective, true ecclesial diversity should not be regarded as an endorsement of parochial identities, but as something that creates the space required for sharing our diverse gifts with each other within the framework of communion. For true and sustainable diversity is always taken up into the service of unity in that it is directed toward building community.

From this several important implications can be drawn regarding the vital question of the proper balance between unity and ecclesial diversity:

1) Since diversity has its limits in the Church's life and one such limit is our obligation to unity, it must be clearly stated that unity is theologically, ecclesiologically, and ecumenically prior to diversity. This definitely does not mean that ecclesial diversity is insignificant to the Church. It does mean, however, that a diversity that conceals and threatens community will cease to function as an enrichment to God's people because it then jeopardizes an even greater gift, namely, God's gift of unity in Christ, a gift not only to the Church but also to the world.

2) This observation also has consequences for the understanding of denominational identities. On the one hand, it would be improper to equate such identities with counterproductive or even illegitimate diversity. On the other hand, the priority of unity indicates that parochial, confessional, and denominational identities are always secondary to the Church's catholicity and its accompanying obligation to communion.

3) When the element of ecclesial diversity is confused either with a static concept that allows the churches to remain "as they are" or with a peaceful coexistence and evident perpetuation of "churches with different confession" (to refer once more to a recent statement on unity by the Evangelical Church in Germany), the limits of constructive and legitimate diversity have been transgressed. Here the capacity

of the Great Tradition of the Church to take us beyond traditional church borders is of vital significance.

4) The best approach to ecclesial diversity is to regard such diversity as a reflection of the many limbs or parts of the one body of the Church. As St. Paul states in 1 Corinthians 12, all parts have immense values provided that they all work for the common good and fulfil their task within the one body.

5) A proper balance between unity and diversity requires an appropriate theology of the Holy Spirit as an indispensable presupposition. For, as noted above, the Spirit both creates and sustains diversity while at the same time holding and knitting our diversities together within the framework of communion.

Pneumatology, however, is not only crucial to the subtle balance between unity and diversity; it is also important when it comes to the *visible* nature of communion. The Holy Spirit, to be sure, has often been presented as a somewhat "floating" or even "airy" entity. Such "spiritualization" of the Spirit, however, represents a misunderstanding of almost disastrous consequences. Quite the contrary, the third Person of the Holy Trinity should be regarded as one of the most concrete and tangible constituents of the Christian faith. This will be discussed in more detail in our deliberations on a "materialist spirituality" in the next chapter. However, the key point is that the Spirit never works in thin air, but through outward and empirically recognizable instruments, chiefly word and sacrament. Moreover, this takes place in a given space, namely, the church where we gather around the means of grace. Now since the Holy Spirit works through visible means, it can be concluded that the communion which is grounded in the activity of the Spirit must be just as visible. Thus the Spirit also emerges as the source and guardian of visible unity. This indicates that our search for an alternative ecumenical concept must start in pneumatology.

A Visible and Structured Community: So that the World May See and Believe

The unity of the Church is given in Christ; we neither can nor shall produce it. However, it is our task to contribute to making this unity visible, to the honor of God and the benefit of all creation. The visible nature of church fellowship is not to be identified with its structural dimensions. Thus it is important to emphasize that all the so-called criteria or requirements of unity discussed above contribute essentially to the visibility of communion, since none of these criteria are in any way invisible. But at the same time it must be maintained that common and mutually binding ecclesial structures play a key role in visualizing unity. These structures aim at serving the Church's unity, holiness, catholicity, and apostolicity as well as its mission in the world. That is the reason why our attempt to present an outline of an alternative ecumenical concept is placed under the rubric "visible and structured community."[22]

Surely church structures are somewhat ambiguous when they are seen in an ecumenical perspective, since many structures are designed primarily to express and protect denominational or parochial institutions. It is necessary to distinguish between structures that pertain to the one church of Christ and denominational structural expressions. As already indicated, such a distinction was introduced by Edmund Schlink when he differentiated between *(bleibende) Grundstrukturen kirchlichen Lebens* ("abiding basic structures of the church's life") and *veränderliche geschichtliche Gestalten der Kirche* ("changing historical shapes of the church"). In concretizing the basic structures, Schlink focused on ecclesiological structures in the history of salvation, ecclesiological structures that pertain to the Church's service, and ecclesiological structures that express the universal unity of the Church.[23] The point of this distinction is not to disregard or overrule every structural form that is historically or denominationally conditioned; such structures also have their relevance and legitimacy. The point is, rather, to make it clear that there are structures that reflect and sustain church fellowship and structures that effectively conceal and jeopardize unity. It is crucial that the latter type of structures never be maintained and perpetuated at the cost of community.

Something must be said about the development of national and confessional structures in the form of "national churches" and international denominational organizations such as the Christian World Communions. We have already noted that according to the New Testament, the church is essentially local and universal. This also applies to church unity. In this perspective, both national and denominational structures must be

---

[22] Without necessarily making explicit use of this concept, I see such texts from the Anglican-Lutheran dialogue as the *Porvoo Common Statement, Called to Common Mission,* and the Canadian *Waterloo Statement,* as well as *Facing Unity* from the Catholic-Lutheran conversations and several of the statements from the Anglican-Roman Catholic International Commission (ARCIC), as fully compatible with "visible structured community."

[23] See Edmund Schlink, *Ökumenische Dogmatik: Grundzüge* (Göttingen: Vandenhoeck & Ruprecht, 1983) 557ff.

understood as secondary to fundamental local and universal structures of the Church and its unity. Such national and denominational structures can only be seen as fully legitimate when they are explicitly intended to contribute to the greater unity that corresponds to the Church's nature. In today's situation, there is a particular need to build structures for universal fellowship, even in the form of a universal ministry of unity.[24]

What kind of structures are we here actually talking about? Several factors are relevant here. Let me limit myself to the following:

1) The structured visibility of church unity corresponds with the structured visibility of the Church itself, in the sense that fellowship between visible church bodies must be visibly embodied. The Church is a body and no mere "idea" or *societas platonica,* and as a body it both has and needs structures. St. Paul's presentation of the Church as Christ's body in 1 Corinthians 12 can implicitly be read as an account of ecclesial and ecumenical structures or as a reflex of the need for such structures.

2) Earlier debates on the relation between structures and charismata, especially those between Christology and pneumatology, have led to an awareness that we are here dealing with perspectives that are, if not identical, at least complementary. They should not be played off against each other. This seems to be affirmed by Hans Küng, who talks explicitly about *a charismatic church structure.*[25]

3) In more concrete terms, church fellowship requires a basically common, if not totally uniform, structure of ordained ministries. The threefold ministerial pattern of the early Church remains a feasible approach. A common ministerial structure will include full interchangeability of ministries, it will provide for concelebration of the Eucharist and possibly also a common episcopate. This would take us far beyond an abstract mutual recognition of ministries.[26]

---

[24] See my brief remarks on the office of the Bishop of Rome on p. 31 above.

[25] See Hans Küng, "Die charismatische Struktur der Kirche," *Concilium* 1 (1965) 282ff. Küng defines a charismatic church structure in a way that is clearly relevant ecumenically: "Charismatisch bestimmte Kirchenordnung bedeutet weder Enthusiasmus, der in Willkür und Unordnung ausartet, noch Gesetzlichkeit, die in Gleichordnung und Uniformität erstarrt. Also weder Willkür noch Uniformität, weder Gleichordnung noch Unordnung, sondern Ordnung in der Freiheit" (288f.).

[26] An example of the problems that may emerge when such a common structure is lacking can be traced in the period since the signing of the *Porvoo Common Statement.* Even if this text provides for full interchangeability of ordained ministries between the participating churches, this does not seem automatically to apply to, for example, the Church of Norway, which continues to allow pastors to be ordained by cathedral deans.

4) When forms of church fellowship have been established, there will be a clear need for binding structures for authoritative teaching and decision-making. This will allow unified churches to speak with one voice, and it will exclude the devastating possibility that a church signs an ecumenical agreement one day and then proceeds to do whatever it wants without consulting with its partners.

5) Finally, ecclesial communion requires common structures for mission and service in the world. This contributes to efficiency in the Church's mission. The most important concern here, however, is that common structures for mission reflect the crucial fact that church unity is not an isolated end in itself, but must always be understood as unity in and for the world. Only in this way can the Church be an effective and credible sign of unity in a deeply divided world.

What is at stake is not some kind of obsession with structures per se. The key point is simply that a divided world—*God's* divided world—may see the Church and its unity and realize that the Church is a stage on the way toward the restoration of the world's own unity. This cannot be achieved through invisible fellowship, static diversity, or mere coexistence. The Church can be a forceful and effective sign of unity in a world marked by militant division and massive discrimination only when its unity is concretely recognizable. Visible unity is crucial to the Church's witness so that people will be able to see and believe (John 17:21). To stress the visibility of community is in harmony with the nature as well as the purpose of the Church. Thus we are summoned to reaffirm our commitment to the goal of visible unity, or more precisely, to the goal of a visibly structured community.

Chapter 5

Life in the Spirit—
Toward a "Materialist" Spirituality

I grew up within the framework of typical Norwegian Lutheran pietism. The personal aspects of the Christian faith were strongly emphasized, as was the exercise of that faith in an individual space that was referred to as *lønnkammeret*, a kind of private or secret chamber. This tradition should obviously not be totally dismissed; our faith surely needs to be personally anchored. Yet many who have been brought up with such piety are today frequently confronted by the painful experience of how difficult it is to practice those ideals. Christian conviction has become increasingly invisible in our daily life. Moreover, the remnants of personal prayer life that still may be left among us are constantly jeopardized by stress and turmoil. Even if I know that I desperately need to pray—simply because for Christians prayer is like breath itself—I must admit that I do this in an ever more fragmented and even accidental way. In short, the tension between our daily existence and the ideals of our piety has become so huge that we tend to lose our piety and all its visible signs. This is largely due to the fact that spirituality is conceived solely in personal or even private terms.

The problem with pietism, and even more with "liberal-pietism," is not only that it has been left without an appropriate ecclesiology; in the final analysis, we are confronted with the fact that these currents in contemporary life seem unable to provide a viable spirituality. And pietism without piety—or a liberal pietism that survives only as a kind of ideology—inevitably emerges at a dead end. To be sure, it must also be admitted that similar problems mark parts of the so-called high church movement, in which there is a tendency to settle for neat ecclesiological theories without realizing that such theories are empty if they do not challenge the way life is lived in Christ and for the world. Actually, spirituality, personal as well as corporate, is to be understood as the space where ecclesiologies are put into practice. So it is that spirituality must be seen as integral to ecclesiological reflection.

It is to be hoped that the previous chapters of this book also suggest impulses toward a viable piety or spirituality. Such spirituality, firmly grounded in the reality of the Church as the body of Christ and the place of salvation, must be communal and collective in nature, transcending mere individualism. This spirituality must be sacramentally anchored, emphasizing the sacraments and particularly the Eucharist as the red thread of Christian life. It must draw from the rich treasures, across time and space, of the Church's faith, be rooted in what we have called the Great Tradition of the Church, and be ecumenically open. (Here Friedrich Heiler's concern, to which we referred earlier, for evangelical focus and catholic breadth is still clearly relevant.) Being directed toward the redemption of God's creation, it must have a taste of earth as well as heaven. Further, growing out of the essential visibility of the Church and the need to make life in Christ empirically recognizable so that the world might believe, this spirituality must be fundamentally visible. This all leads to what is here to be called a "materialist spirituality."

A Spirituality for Today—
Vague and Evasive or Physical and Palpable?

While the very notion of spirituality was, three or four decades ago, often considered somewhat obsolete, such is not the case today. To the contrary, there is widespread interest in what is called "the spiritual sphere." This can perhaps be seen as a good thing; it may at least have contributed to an increase in the "market value" of Christianity. Yet we need to take a closer and more critical view of the *type* of spirituality that has gained popular acclaim.

The following features seem to be central:

1) Contemporary spiritualities are marked by an almost boundless plurality as well as by subsequent esoteric vagueness and elusiveness.

2) There is a strong sensitivity for what can be "sold" at the religious marketplace, and so it is that spirituality has been turned into a commodity produced for private consumption, much like other goods.

3) Such spirituality is basically therapeutic inasmuch as it is designed primarily to increase the well-being of individuals, with little attention to the needs of fellow humans or the world.

4) Even if many churches are eager to borrow from popular contemporary spiritualities, these currents largely live their lives outside the established churches or other forms of traditional religion. Within Christianity, it is probably the neo-charismatic movement that has been most successful in responding to popular demands.

5) Finally, what we see today is a radically privatized spirituality. People are refusing to accept ready-made creedal systems, choosing instead to invent their own religion. This attitude has had notable consequences in the "folk churches" of Northern Europe, which contain vast numbers of people who share the churches' faith only to a very modest degree.[1]

Spiritualities of these kinds have become major factors in today's religious market and increasingly are also being embraced, with considerable impact, in the lives of churches. Yet these attitudes deviate radically from what can be characterized as genuine or traditional Christian spirituality. One can even argue that contemporary spiritualities have more in common with the kind of gnostic spirituality vehemently opposed by the early Church than with the authentic tradition of the Church. Instead of this predominantly esoteric, consumerist, and privatized spirituality, the Church through the ages has been dedicated to that which is plain or even simple, to that which is not designed to be sold but rather offered freely, to that which is collective or communal in nature. This can be found in the ecclesial spirituality of such early church fathers as Irenaeus or Cyprian, in different forms of monastic spirituality, in Martin Luther's strong emphasis on the outward Word, in sacramentally and eucharistically based piety, and in more recent "earthly" or creation-oriented spirituality. All these currents are characterized by the fact that they are anchored in concrete, palpable, and empirically recognizable things.[2] They emerge as the opposite of evasive and vague spiritualities, or as an expression of what I label, perhaps somewhat paradoxically, a "materialist" spirituality and piety.

Let me make a first attempt to define this materialist spirituality, or at least to identify some of its central features in more detail. Such a piety originates in a specific place, the Church; it has a language of its

[1] Some of these points are documented in an important work by Eva M. Hamberg, *Studies in the Prevalence of Religious Beliefs and Religious Practice in Contemporary Sweden*, Ph.D. thesis, Acta Universitatis Upsaliensis. Psychologia et Sociologia Religionum 4 (Uppsala: Scripta Academiae Upsaliensis, 1990).

[2] See Cheslyn Jones, Geoffrey Wainwright, and Edward Yarnold, S.J., eds., *The Study of Spirituality* (London: SPCK, 1986).

own, liturgy; it is sacramentally based with the external and visible means of grace as its backbone; it applies primarily to the life of God's people as a whole and only through this community to each person as an individual; it is not directed toward producing nice religious sentiments or feelings, but is expressed through what we *do* and the concrete signs that accompany life in Christ; and it is firmly grounded in both creation and redemption. Here the necessary and firm framework for the Christian life can be located. Here persons pray together and are carried by the prayers of the community of the faithful across both time and space. Here personal Christian witness is integrated into the witness of the Church as a whole.

These are main ingredients of a materialist spirituality that is basically identical with an ecclesial or ecclesially anchored spirituality. The nagging feeling of being left alone that often comes out of traditional pietism is counteracted by a spirituality that realizes, in the words of John Donne, that "no man is an island" and that "we do not live to ourselves, and we do not die to ourselves" (Rom 14:7). Moreover, this kind of piety not only corresponds to the nature and purpose of the Church; it also pays due attention to the world, aiming at responding to its needs. A materialist spirituality represents a far more appropriate answer to the needs of all human beings in their feeble search for a vibrant spiritual life than the alternatives that are offered in the contemporary, confusing religious marketplace. It emerges as a highly significant contribution toward filling the spiritual vacuum that haunts people today.

The Holy Spirit: Foundation of a Materialist Spirituality

The call and the desire to live a life in the Holy Spirit are at the core of all Christian spiritualities, a sign of the crucial role of the third Person of the Trinity in Christian life. Among the biblical accounts of such a life, Galatians 5:16ff. is of particular relevance. The main focus in this passage is on factors such as love, peace, patience, kindness, and gentleness, factors that are signs of plain human decency as well as "ecumenical" deeds that promote unity and solidarity. In contrast, the destructive and egocentric "desires of the flesh" exclude an authentically spiritual life. Today, however, we often witness approaches in which the Spirit is "spiritualized" beyond recognition.[3] The Spirit is

---

[3] Obviously, the aim of this brief paragraph is no more than to make an observation concerning the role of the Holy Spirit within the framework of a materialist spirituality.

further "anthropologized" when it is identified with or absorbed by human religious experience or sentiments. This may be seen as a consequence of the downplaying of the Holy Spirit in the theology and practice of many mainline churches, in contrast to neo-charismatic movements. Such downplaying has resulted in a picture of the Spirit as vague and elusive, a pneumatology that resembles the spiritualities of the religious marketplace.

This development is regrettable in that it has obscured the nature and task of God the Holy Spirit. As the one who mediates and applies salvation in the lives of the faithful, the Spirit should rather be seen as the source of true "earthly" spirituality. One might even speak of a materialist pneumatology. This may be made specific by pointing to five crucial factors:

1) The Spirit is to be seen primarily as a *person* of the Holy Trinity and not as some kind of expression or reflection of human religious sentiments.

2) The key task of the Holy Spirit is to be the spokesperson who points to Christ; the Spirit is the one who mediates the presence of the risen Christ in the midst of the assembly. The Spirit is therefore where Christ is.

3) The work of the Holy Spirit in mediating Christ does not occur in thin air. This work is done through outward, empirically recognizable means—word and sacrament—and in a particular place, the Church. This ecclesial focus does not necessarily limit the work of the Spirit to the Church; the Spirit is also the Spirit of creation, the *ruah* who animates God's creatures (Gen 1). Yet the main task of the Spirit is to mediate salvation in Christ, and this takes place in the Church.

4) The Holy Spirit is the Spirit of communion, keeping the limbs of Christ's body together (1 Cor 12) and joining all in a living fellowship in which the law of Christ is fulfilled as each other's burdens are borne (Gal 6:2).

5) As *Spiritus Creator*, the Spirit of creation, the Holy Spirit also points toward the ultimate liberation and restoration of God's creation.

We are not able to reflect on pneumatology in its totality here. However, two important books that have made valuable contributions to this area of study should be mentioned: Yves Congar, *Der Heilige Geist* (Freiburg: Herder, 1982), and Karl Rahner, *The Spirit in the Church*, trans. John Griffiths and W. J. O'Hara (London: Search Press; New York: Seabury Press, 1979). These two works bear witness to the importance of pneumatology in recent Roman Catholic theology.

Accordingly, to reduce pneumatology to the level of individual experience is radically to devaluate the Spirit's role.

Such is the pneumatology of the Great Tradition of the Church and
also of the Lutheran Reformation.[4] This is affirmed, although somewhat negatively, by Luther's stern criticism of the "enthusiasts" of the
radical Reformation, who, according to Luther, jeopardized a proper
understanding of the Holy Spirit by putting God's inward work in
heart and soul before his outward work through the means of grace.
More positive is the substance of Article V of the Augsburg Confession
(AC), where it is stated that justification before God and participation
in the fruits of Christ's sacrifice are mediated by the Holy Spirit through
word and sacrament in the Church and by the service of the publicly
ordained ministry. We have earlier argued that this view reflects the
true catholicity of the Reformation.

This indicates that the claim that Western Christianity in general
and the Lutheran Reformation in particular have no adequate theology of the Holy Spirit depends either on a misunderstanding or on a
clearly biased pneumatology which denies that the Spirit works through
outward means. It must be admitted, however, that the pneumatology
of AC Article V virtually vanished in the post-Reformation period.
This began in a certain sense as early as the time of Lutheran Orthodoxy, but it became dominant in the narrow christomonism of pietism
and liberal theology. A somewhat similar development can be traced
within the Roman Catholic Church, where massive christomonist institutionalism occasionally threatened to dispel or even destroy pneumatology. Because of such developments, necessary and explicit
pneumatological reflection has often been left largely to various representatives of the charismatic movement.

In this light one may argue that both Western Christianity at large
and the churches of the Lutheran Reformation in particular need to
renew their theology of the Holy Spirit or, rather, need to retrieve their
authentic pneumatology. Much can be learned from the deep insight
concerning and commitment to the Holy Spirit found in the charismatic
movement. However, the early Church and the Orthodox tradition of
the East have the most to offer with regard to theological substance.

---

[4] With regard to the pneumatology of the Lutheran Reformation in general and Martin Luther in particular, see the excellent study by Regin Prenter, *Spiritus Creator*, trans.
John M. Jensen (Philadelphia: Muhlenberg Press, 1953).

Under all circumstances, any tendency in ecclesiological reflection to play pneumatology off against christology must be avoided. As indicated above in Chapter 3 (pp. 43ff.), an appropriate theology of the Church presupposes that Christology and pneumatology are held firmly together in a dynamic dialectic in which the christological dimension is seen as the point of departure. This becomes particularly important for a materialist pneumatology that differs radically from a falsely spiritualized concept by means of its inclusion of concrete ecclesial and sacramental elements. Seen in this perspective, pneumatology is more relevant in relation to an ecclesially based spirituality than it is to the quest for appropriate church structures.

Word and Sacraments as Core, Liturgy as Language

Some brief remarks on the fundamental connection, the dialectic, between word and sacraments are required here. First, the Lutheran Reformers explicitly adopted the basically Augustinian description of the sacrament as *verbum visibile* ("visible word"). Second, by emphasizing the external word and its immediate power, the Reformers came close to a sacramental perception of the Word of God. Third, despite differences in scope and aim, the Reformers posited a basic interaction between all the means of grace, a clear implication that none of these means can be neglected. Attempts to play word and sacrament off against each other must be rejected, especially in relation to Christian spirituality.[5]

An appropriate point of departure for an exploration of sacramentality and the individual sacraments is the "sign theology" of Augustine, found especially in his arguments against the Donatists, who held that only sacraments administered by truly faithful priests could be regarded as valid. This sign theology was adopted and further developed by the Lutheran Reformers. Sacraments, in this view, are seen as consisting of two things: the sacramental sign or element and God's promise in Christ, *signum* and *res*, the sign and the thing itself. These two entities should neither be confused nor torn completely apart. God's promise is the core of the sacrament, yet the promise can be implemented and fulfilled only through the sign and not in some spiritualized vacuum.

Thus the sacramental gifts are available only through the *signa*, the elements. The grace of baptism always comes with baptismal water; the

---

[5] On the Word in a wider pneumatological perspective, see Yves Congar, *The Word and the Spirit* (London: Geoffrey Chapman, 1986).

gifts of the Eucharist, through eating and drinking; and the forgiveness that follows penitence, through the spoken Word of God and the laying on of hands. For Martin Luther, this was theologically as well as pastorally crucial: the tormented soul should not look at his or her deeds or feelings, but should rather cling to both the empirically recognizable sacramental elements and the external word. The sacraments, or the means of grace, accordingly emerge as the core of a materialist spirituality. By emphasizing that grace is not an abstract idea or a feeling, but rather a most concrete thing that is mediated through the outward word, through the water of baptism, and through what is eaten at the eucharistic table, spirituality is provided with a sound empirical foundation. It must be emphasized here that faith is not constitutive of the sacraments as such, but it is an instrument necessary or required for the reception of the sacramental gift. In point of fact, a kind of circular argument is applicable here, an argument in harmony with AC Article XIII: the faith that is essential for the reception of the sacramental gifts is actually given through the sacraments as a kind of *creatio ex nihilo*.

The central sacraments, baptism and the Eucharist, have a key role to play in this spirituality. Baptism is the *prima porta gratiae et ecclesiae* ("the first gate to grace and the church"), and the Lord's Supper is a celebration of our participation in the fruits of Christ's sacrificial offering and the continual nourishment of life in him. Roman Catholics accept this special emphasis without limiting themselves to two or three sacraments. They identify seven sacramental acts, including, in addition to baptism and the Eucharist, confirmation, penance, ordination or holy orders, marriage, and the anointing of the sick. The sacraments, therefore, can be said to surround or encircle human existence from its feeble beginning until its end; they are the red thread of both life in Christ and a materialist spirituality.[6] This reinforces what has been claimed earlier about the sacramental character of the Church as such and its service as *sacramentum mundi*, a sacrament in and for the world. It can be argued that the difference between Roman Catholic and Lutheran approaches to the number of the sacraments is not a matter of distinct theologies but rather of wider and narrower sacramental con-

---

[6] Concerning a sacramentally based spirituality, see Alexander Schmemann, *For the Life of the World: Sacraments and Orthodoxy* (Crestwood, N.Y.: St. Vladimir's Seminary Press, 1988). A challenging exposition of what may be called "earthly sacramentality" can be found in Leonardo Boff, *Sacraments of Life: Life of the Sacraments* (Washington: Pastoral Press, 1987).

cepts. This point seems to be confirmed, as we have already noted, in Philipp Melanchthon's "wider" sacramental concept as found in Article XIII of his Apology of the Augsburg Confession (1531).

Since the celebration of all sacraments takes place within a liturgical framework, a sacramental spirituality will be liturgically anchored.[7] As has been pointed out, liturgical prayer and worship can be described as the main language of the Church, the body of Christ. This language has always played a crucial role in both the Great Tradition of the Church and in the movement of evangelical catholicity. Further, the language of liturgy is in three respects a vital constituent of materialist spirituality.

1) Liturgy and its language are corporeal or bodily rather than intellectual. Liturgy aims at holding divine action and human acts together; in other words, God's action is connected with the things worshipers *do* in the liturgy. Among such things are the making of the sign of the cross, gestures like kneeling, bowing, and standing, and a rich variety of musical expression. These human acts are not merely pedagogical matters into which theological meaning is rather desperately squeezed. The outward acts actually carry the inward meaning. As for liturgical music, this is implicitly affirmed by Augustine's famous statement *qui cantat bis orat* ("the one who sings prays twice as strongly").

2) The collective nature of liturgy also contributes significantly to materialist spirituality. Within the framework of liturgical worship, God deals primarily with his people as a whole or a body, not as individuals. This is expressed, for example, when the priest "collects" the prayers of the faithful and includes them in the prayers of the church (the Collect). It therefore makes little sense to evaluate the service of worship on the basis of more or less private criteria; the key concern is rather that which serves and builds up the body of Christ as a whole.

3) Just as life in the Church is life in and for the world, liturgy must also be directed toward the Church's task as *sacramentum mundi*. What is at stake in liturgical celebration is not a matter of isolated aesthetic

---

[7] In this account I owe much to Professor Paul DeClerck of the Institut Supérieur de Liturgie in Paris, especially for his paper "A Catholic Understanding of Liturgy" and our personal conversations. He should, however, not be held responsible for my reflections. See also the classic expositions of Gregory Dix, *The Shape of the Liturgy*, 2nd ed. (London: A & C Black, 1986), and Louis Bouyer, *Life and Liturgy* (London: Sheed and Ward, 1956). The recent work of Gordon Lathrop is also important: *Holy Things: A Liturgical Theology* (Minneapolis: Fortress Press, 1993) and *Holy People: A Liturgical Ecclesiology* (Minneapolis: Fortress Press, 1999); a third volume on liturgical cosmology is forthcoming.

concern but preparation for mission. It must be clearly manifest in liturgical worship that the assembly gathers on behalf of God's entire creation; it is called to carry the world to God in its prayers.

In general terms, the service of worship can be understood as an ellipsis with two central points: Christ's sacrifice and our responding *sacrificium*, a response that brings about effective change. The liturgy is directed toward a twofold transformation fundamental to Christian life. The first transformation is of mind and spirit, a transformation that takes place through specific outward acts. The Rule of St. Benedict is pertinent to this in its emphasis on the aim of the liturgy to tune the worshipers' minds into harmony with their voices: *ut mens nostra concordet voci nostrae*. It is our minds that are supposed to be tuned into harmony with our voices, not the other way round. In this perspective it is clear that the concrete acts or signs that accompany or at least *should* accompany liturgical celebration play a far more vital role than Protestants normally assume. The second transformation is just as essential: the transformation of individual believers into the Body of Christ. Indeed, it can be argued that God transforms individuals into a body precisely through communal liturgical acts. All this leads to the conclusion that the liturgy of the Church is incarnational, concrete, and collective.

The goal of the liturgy is to "re-create" the mystery of faith as expressed in the paschal drama. While liturgy is of fundamental significance in regard to both theology and doctrine, it is clearly more than abstract theology. Liturgy is lived, implemented, and enacted theology. For this reason liturgical celebration can even be perceived as a "performance." In liturgy the principle of *lex orandi lex credendi* is validated ("the law of prayer is the law of faith"). The description of "liturgical theology" offered by David Fagerberg is most helpful at this point:

> The subject matter of liturgical theology is not liturgy, it is God, humanity and the world, and the vortex in which these three essentially entangle is liturgy. If the subject matter of liturgical theology were human ceremony instead of God, it would be sheer self-delusion to call it theology; it would be anthropology, not theology. Liturgy is theological precisely because here is where God's revelation occurs steadfastly . . . (T)he meaning of the liturgy, its *lex orandi*, is ultimately the Church's faith enacted, i.e., symbolized, but it does not exist in naked vertical forms, either as proposition or as emotion. Vertical, pneumatic Tradition projects itself onto the historical line and is manifested in Scripture, liturgies, icons, and dogmas where these sources function precisely as sources. Liturgical theology searches for the code presupposed by the whole con-

tent of what is encoded in its liturgy. It searches for the *lex orandi* which establishes *lex credendi* encodents.[8]

Materialist Spirituality as Eucharistic Spirituality

In comparison with today's blooming religious market, a eucharistically based and directed spirituality may come across as rather trivial and unexciting. How can a tiny wafer and a small amount of wine be endowed with such a crucial role for our life in Christ? Questions such as this have led many to a frantic search for "stronger" religious experience.

In this situation the key challenge is to show people that the Church's eucharistic celebration actually does reflect and contain the mystery of faith in the fullest sense. This is the place where the threads of life in Christ are gathered. The Eucharist emerges as the core not only of what is here called materialist spirituality but of the spirituality that has been advocated through the ages by classical Christianity, the Great Tradition of the Church. The following paragraphs will try to elaborate this point further by a brief presentation of some vital aspects of the Church's eucharistic tradition and its corresponding "spirituality of the table."

1) Our Lord Jesus Christ, the Lamb of God, is both the host and the food at the eucharistic table; without him there is no Eucharist. The Lord's Supper can be characterized as the sacrament of Christ's presence par excellence. He is the one who invites to the table; he prepares the meal; and he is the Bread of Life offered and consumed at the table. In this way grace is mediated through the ordinary and common acts of eating and drinking; the event is not to be spiritualized. Here sacramental memory, or *anamnesis,* plays a crucial role. Yet the celebration of the Eucharist in remembrance of Christ is not to be understood either in emotional or intellectual terms. Rather, the point is that Christ's unique sacrificial offering at the cross is made sacramentally present in a most concrete manner when the Eucharist is celebrated. Furthermore, even if this offering cannot be repeated and does not require repetition, it makes no sense at all to reduce it to a past historical incident or episode. To the contrary, the sacrifice of Calvary is made present and alive when the sacrament of the *anamnesis* of Christ is celebrated.

2) When Christ is encountered at the eucharistic table, his presence is full and real. He is present as true man and true God, as the

---

[8] David Fagerberg, *What Is Liturgical Theology? A Study in Methodology* (Collegeville, Minn.: The Liturgical Press, 1992) 10, 301.

earthly Jesus and the risen Christ, with all his gifts. This is the central point of the doctrine of the Real Presence; it is at the core of the Great Tradition of the Church as well as of authentic Lutheran theology. The Real Presence is really real! Whether we choose to describe this presence by use of the traditional Roman Catholic theory of transubstantiation, which indicates that the bread and wine keep their outward characteristics while being transformed in their inner substance, or the Lutheran view that Christ's body and blood are given in, with, and under the shape of bread and wine, this choice makes little difference.

It must, however, be maintained that conviction about this presence cannot be reduced to some kind of figurative or metaphorical concept. The point is not only that we eat and drink Christ, without ending up in a "Capernaistic" misunderstanding, but that by such eating and drinking we actually become the body of Christ. This is the point of St. Paul when in 1 Corinthians 12, in an astonishingly concrete manner, he identifies the not particularly flawless congregation in Corinth with Christ's body. Moreover, when we pray the *Agnus Dei*, the prayer is directed not only to the one who sits at the right hand of the Father but also to Christ at the altar, the one who comes to us through bread and wine.

It has been pointed out more than once in the foregoing that this doctrine of the Real Presence played a key role in the theology of the Lutheran Reformers, Martin Luther in particular. As an example of this, it is perhaps more instructive to point out that Luther was fully prepared to excommunicate priests who through their theology and practice put the Real Presence in jeopardy, than to focus on the famous incidents when Luther knelt to lick up spilled wine. Again, reference to his stern reaction to the two pastors Wolferinus and Besserer in the turbulent 1540s should be made. While it appears to have been an accident that Besserer placed consecrated and unconsecrated hosts together, Wolferinus defended that practice theologically by insisting that the Real Presence applied only to the *actio sacramentalis,* the sacramental act itself. Although Besserer did only what the vast majority of Lutheran pastors do today every time they celebrate the Eucharist, both of these priests were excommunicated by Luther for their accommodation to a "Zwinglian heresy." Luther preferred that consecrated elements be either consumed or kept separately for later use.[9]

⁹ As already indicated, this is forcefully documented in Jürgen Diestelmann, *Actio Sacramentalis: Die Verwaltung des Heiligen Abendmahls nach den Prinzipien Martin Luthers in*

All this suggests that there is a radical disconnection at this point between Luther and contemporary Lutheranism. It can well be argued that although the Real Presence is still maintained as a general theological idea by Lutherans, an awareness of the need to concretely visualize the Real Presence in the celebration of the Eucharist and the handling of the elements has largely been lost. Today Luther's eucharistic practice would probably be dismissed by a vast number of Lutherans as being "too Catholic." Such persons apparently have more in common with Besserer and even Wolferinus, even though both these pastors were excommunicated.

The reality of this difference between Luther and many Lutherans also has clear ecumenical implications. While Luther insisted that *ehe ich mit den schwermern wolt eytel wein haben, so wolt ich ehe mit dem Papst eytel blut haben* ("rather than drink pure wine with the fanatics, I would prefer to drink pure blood with the Pope"),[10] many of his followers today seem to be far more inclined to drink wine with the Protestants than blood with the Pope. I am convinced that many parts of Martin Luther's eucharistic practice remained densely Catholic. It is crucial to regain and visualize this practice, not only at the level of theological abstraction but especially in concrete sacramental celebration.

3) As at other tables, the main gift at the Lord's table is food. However, we are not here talking about ordinary perishable food, but about food that never perishes, Christ the Bread of Life. Through this bread forgiveness of sins is received, and participation in and with Christ is made possible. It has already been noted that the Real Presence is at the core of the Eucharist, but this crucial concern should not be emphasized in an isolated or one-sided way. Along with the Real Presence of Christ, many other gifts are presented within the framework of eucharistic celebration: the Eucharist involves thanksgiving to the Father and prayer for both the Church and the world; it is the most transparent

---

der Zeit bis zur Konkordienformel (Gross Oesingen: H. Harms, 1996). In this important study the cases of Besserer and Wolferinus are presented along with several other examples of what might be described as Luther's Catholic eucharistic practice. Not only the duration of the sacramental presence and an appropriate understanding of the principle of *in usu* are stressed in this work, but Luther's insistence that the words of institution are words of consecration, his understanding of the practice of elevation, his requirement of *Nachkonsekration*, when new bread and wine are brought to the eucharistic table, etc., are also emphasized as crucial to his eucharistic spirituality.

[10] Weimar Ausgabe (WA), *Martin Luthers Werke, Kritische Ausgabe*, 26, 462, 1ff.

manifestation of the Church; it includes *epiklesis,* or invocation of the Holy Spirit, a concern totally in keeping with Lutheran theology in general and AC Article V in particular; it provides a most appropriate context for the presentation of human bodies as a living sacrifice to God; and it serves as a foundation and visualization of mutual Christian love and solidarity. Thus it is that the Eucharist emerges as a celebration of the mystery of faith in all its fullness.

4) The Eucharist is the sacrament of communion—*koinonia.* This communion is a participation in the life of the Holy Trinity through Christ and in the Spirit. However, this vertical *koinonia* points immediately toward a horizontal fellowship between all the faithful across time and space. These two aspects of Christian communion cannot be torn apart: fellowship with Christ includes fellowship with all the people of God and vice versa. Such double communion is or should be expressed in a particularly direct manner at the eucharistic table. In the early Church this horizontal or social dimension of the Eucharist was made immediate by the accompanying "agape meal." Moreover, liturgies remind us that the eucharistic celebration comprises the faithful in heaven as well as on earth. Today, however, such concerns tend to be less and less visible, and, indeed, the Eucharist has become individualized and privatized almost beyond recognition. There are often few if any signs of real social fellowship and solidarity in the way communicants gather around the Lord's table. This is yet another aspect of eucharistic spirituality that needs to be regained and revived in churches.

As the sacrament of *koinonia,* the Eucharist serves as a constant pointer to the unity of all God's people in one visible body. Every time the Eucharist is celebrated we are summoned to an affirmation of commitment to this goal of unity. However, there are, as already indicated, two errors that must be avoided. On the one hand, there is an "all or nothing" approach which suggests that there is *only* full communion or no communion at all. In contrast to this view, it must be maintained that all efforts to realize eucharistic fellowship are part of a process that involves different steps and stages. At each of these stages various provisional forms of fellowship (communion) may be possible. On the other hand, the proclivity to confuse the goal of unity with steps toward that goal is strong. The fact that the Eucharist is a celebration of the mystery of faith in its totality and the primary manifestation of the Church as a whole means that full unity at the Lord's table must be perceived as the goal of ecumenism rather than as a means to achieve that goal. Eucharistic hospitality, so called, requires substantial unity in eucharistic faith as well as in practice.[11]

5) The bread and wine of the eucharistic table and its tangible implications are not to be seen merely as pedagogical devices or fancy illustrations. They are, rather, concrete pointers to the world. This concern has several important consequences. First, it reminds us that the aim of the church is not only that souls should be saved but that God's creation is to be redeemed. Second, it points to the Eucharist as the eschatological meal that serves as an anticipatory sign of God's kingdom in its fullness. Third, from the eucharistic table persons are sent into the world in order to share bread with all those who suffer from hunger and deprivation, simply because those who have benefited from Christ's boundless love and solidarity are committed to show the same to others. To depict the Eucharist as some sort of cozy internal event or as an opportunity for "religious" escape, a private tryst with God, is clearly in error. On the contrary, the earthly spirituality expressed in the Eucharist holds church and world together.

The Visible Nature of Christian Spirituality

The materialist spirituality described here should not be perceived merely as an attempt to correct contemporary "spiritualized" spiritualities. Our point has rather been to draw upon the rich sources for Christian piety that have evolved within the Great Tradition of the Church. Such a spirituality grows out of an emphasis on the visible nature of the Church, a crucial concern of this book. The visible church and its equally visible communion are expressed through visible ecclesial life and piety. Further, this visible spirituality as anchored in the world and directed toward fellow humans reveals once more what the Church's visibility is all about. We are not at all concerned here with some kind of "high church" fancy for ecclesial structures. What is at stake is simply that people be able *to see* the Church as an anticipation of God's kingdom, *to see* the Church's unity as a powerful sign of reconciliation for a divided world, *to see* the life of this church as an

---

[11] These issues are discussed in *Christen wollen das eine Abendmahl* (Mainz: Grünewald Verlag, 1971), a volume that includes contributions by Heinrich Bacht, Peter Brunner, Walter Kasper, Alfons Kirchgässer, Karl Lehmann, and Wolfhart Pannenberg. In this connection, see also *Intercommunion: The Report of the Theological Commission Appointed by the Continuation Committee of the World Conference on Faith and Order* (London: SCM Press, 1952). At present, there is an intense debate on these questions in Germany.

expression of life in its fullness, and on the basis of such sight *to believe.* To be sure, when people view the Church, they also encounter nasty stuff, for the Church is both God's creation and an entity that shares in the brokenness of the human community. Yet under these circumstances we are not to attempt to hide the Church by insisting on its invisibility. We are rather called by the ambiguous reality of the Church to do our utmost in faithfulness to God's calling in Christ. That is precisely what a visible spiritual life intends.

Some of the key concerns of this concluding chapter should be repeated.

1) A materialist spirituality is rooted in the work of concrete persons: the Father who calls, the Son who liberates, and the Spirit who leads into a new life.

2) A materialist spirituality has a physical substance: the external word and visible sacraments with empirically recognizable elements.

3) A materialist spirituality has a specific space or *locus:* the church where spiritual life is born and nourished.

4) A materialist spirituality has the capacity to release persons from the temptation of private religious consumption, summoning them rather to communal life. Such life is based on *koinonia* with the Father through the Son and in the Spirit, and it is lived within a fellowship with all the faithful across time and space.

5) A materialist spirituality is earthbound in that it is lived in God's world and in mission to all God's creatures.

Finally, let us again affirm that life in the Spirit is not to be identified with some kind of secluded or insular "religious" existence. This life is rather to be seen as fundamental to the restoration of "normal" life and to the realization of true humanity as intended by God the Creator. This is what is meant when Christian life is described as "life in its fullness." Such life is dedicated to the glory of God and to the benefit of every human being and all creation. Christ is the one who sets us free to live such a life. And that life is always lived in the power of the Holy Spirit.

Postscript

Some readers may feel that the present book is marked by a predominantly critical, perhaps even bluntly negative perspective. Admittedly, there are things and currents in the field of ecclesiology that I view as requiring a thorough examination and reevaluation. Nevertheless, I would like to underline the fact that my chief intention is positive and constructive. Let me make this concrete by means of some concluding points that I hope will also help gather whatever loose ends may remain.

First, my key aim has been to offer a glimpse of the vast richness that marks the life and witness of the Church across time and space in accordance with "the Great Tradition." Since this richness is firmly grounded in God's gifts to his people through Christ and in the Spirit, it can be blurred and concealed, though never destroyed or terminated, by the distressing fact that the Church also shares in the brokenness of human community. This conviction corresponds with God's promise in Christ that the powers of death and evil shall never prevail over the life of the *una sancta.* Even if there is perhaps not so much that we *must* believe concerning the Church for the sake of salvation, there is surely much that we *can* and *should* believe, simply because it will be an immense enrichment.

Second, there are several paths to the Church's richness, primarily Holy Scripture together with the witness of the ancient Church. However, in this book an additional option has been explored: the path of ecumenism. Here the Church's experience across time and space and across denominational and cultural borders is unfolded in a most convincing, almost breathtaking manner. Moreover, we are invited into a living communion in which we participate in the life of the Holy Trinity and share in one another's gifts—real gifts, not requirements of formal or juridical validity. This is the main rationale of an *ecumenical* way of doing ecclesiology. It is also the chief reason why I consider the approach to unity that operates with neat "least common denominators" to be ecumenically counterproductive. This is based on a conviction that ecumenism is supposed to make us richer, not poorer.

Third, the ultimate goal of the Church and the *communio* we participate in is not only that souls shall be saved but that God's creation shall be redeemed and humanity reunified. This goal cannot be fulfilled if we settle for a basically invisible or falsely spiritualized church. To the contrary, the church that is called to be the priest of creation and the First-fruit of a reunited humankind must be concretely visible and empirically recognizable in order that people may see the rich gifts that God has entrusted to the Church and thus may believe. One may argue that richness and visibility are two sides of the same coin. Generally, the Church's visibility is derived from the empirically visible factors that constitute it. It extends to its existence as human fellowship and spiritual community, offering a visible life marked by a "materialist" spirituality.

In order to round off the whole argument, I would like again to stress that being in Christ is life in fullness. However, such a life cannot be reduced to abstractions, internal feelings, or to an individual adherence to a certain set of beliefs; rather, this full life is born, nourished, and maintained in a corporate way and in a specific place or location. And this place is the Church. Clearly this does not mean that the Church is to be seen as the provider of salvation. Only Christ can save, but the Church is his body in a most real sense. Accordingly, the Church emerges as the place where we participate in the fruits of Christ's sacrificial offering at Calvary through word and sacrament and where we enjoy *koinonia* with, or participation in, the life of the Holy Trinity. In this sense there is much truth to the old saying *extra ecclesiam nulla salus*. As I see it, the concept of "place" is far more appropriate than a purely functional perception of the Church's role as the instrument of salvation. In this a sacramentally based ecclesiology plays a key role. And beneath all this lies the conviction that the Church is a reflex of the most beautiful thing that can be envisioned, namely, the one who gives his life for the many.

My main problem with "liberal-pietistic" Protestantism, as well as with a significant number of the opinions that are labeled "Lutheran" today, is that these currents fall considerably short of all the crucial concerns I have mentioned. This is partly a result of traditional Protestant minimalism and reductionism that increasingly comes through as a project of bereavement. It also stems, however, from the more recent—one might fashionably say "postmodern"—attitude that makes concession to a limitless, vague, and highly static pluralism whose main concern is that the churches shall "remain as they are," without either change or even a desire to learn from sisters and brothers in Christ. Such currents have almost nothing in common with authentic Lutheran theology. We could even say that at best the original catholicity and ecumenicity of the Reformation is now a clearly endangered species within contemporary Lutheranism; at worst, it has been marginalized beyond rescue.

In this situation we are forced to face most serious questions: Where should "catholic" Lutherans go? What are our options? Where do we belong, not least in terms of our worship life? I still have the greatest respect and admiration for the founding fathers as well as today's leaders of the movement for "evangelical catholicity" in its different forms. However, I cannot escape the nagging feeling that this movement is meaningful only to a notably decreasing number of individuals, and almost never to the churches as such. Moreover, the ongoing marginalization of evangelical catholicity within Lutheranism has taken place with immense speed. In some churches, especially on the European scene, one is almost tempted to ask the last one to leave to turn off the lights. Surely life is too short to fight to preserve what may prove to be little more than a castle in the air.

In the final analysis, I do not see much more than two feasible options here: either an insistence on "the Great Tradition of the Church," which is increasingly being manifested and maintained *across* traditional denominational borders. However, this approach will require that especially the Roman Catholic Church and the Orthodox churches respond positively to those who share their faith without being able to become formal members of these churches. It remains hard to see what such a solution will mean ecclesiologically and in terms of church membership. The other option is conversion, in many ways emerging as a defeat, but still as a path that more and more people feel pushed into. To be homeless in the place that was supposed to be our home on earth is deeply painful, particularly so when one is forced to celebrate the Eucharist in a way that deviates notably from what one would perceive as a proper celebration of the sacrament.

I have already made it clear that I have chosen the path of conversion to the Roman Catholic Church. This decision, however, is marked not only by a break but also by a significant measure of continuity. My main concern is to live out my commitment to the Great Tradition in a new, and in my view more appropriate, setting. Yet I have the greatest respect for those who decide to stay and fight. I shall in a sense probably always remain an "evangelical catholic." I also hope to be an "ecumenical convert" who is firmly committed to the *una sancta* and the vision of visible unity. So help me God.

Index

Aalen, Leiv, 7n6
Adorno, Theodor, 17
anamnesis, 105
Assmussen, Hans, 22
Augsburg Confession, 3, 4, 8, 11, 12, 13, 14, 23, 25, 53, 56, 57, 82, 100, 103
Augustine, St., ix, 28, 47, 103
    Donatists and, 101
Aulén, Gustaf, 23n2

Bach, Johann Sebastian, 15
Bacht, Heinrich, 109n11
baptism. *See* sacrament(s).
Beaupère, René, 80, 80n10
Benestad, Finn, 15n13
Bernard of Clairvaux, St., 35
Besserer, 13, 13n12, 106, 107
Best, Thomas F., 60n19
Bexell, Peter, 42n3
Bildersturm. See iconoclasm.
Birmele, André, 83n16
bishop(s), 30–1, 57–8
Boff, Leonardo, 102n6
Bonhoeffer, Dietrich, 70n29
Bouyer, Louis, 42n3, 103n7
Braaten, Carl E., xin1, 4n4, 22n1, 41n1, 56n16, 64n22, 67n27
Brilioth, Yngve, 23n2
Brodd, Sven-Erik, 22n1
Brown, Peter, 66n24

Brunner, Peter, 109n11
Bugenhagen, Johannes, 6, 67
Burgess, Joseph A., 3n2, 83n16

Called to Common Mission (1999), 75
Church. *See also* Great Tradition of the Church.
    apostolicity and the, 67–9
    attributes/marks of the, 64–9
    fellowship in the, 86–7, 88
    Great Tradition of the, 21–2, 27–37
    invisibility vs. visibility of the, xviii, 70–1, 75–80, 93, 96, 109–10
    justification and the, 50–4
    membership in the, 33–4
    pluralism and the, 75–7, 83
    salvation and the, 50
    secularized activism and the, 61, 63
    structures. *See* ecclesiology.
Church of England, 33
Church of Norway, 9, 33, 84
Collins, John, 59n17
Congar, Yves, 43n4, 59n18, 80n11, 98n3, 101n5
conversion, xii, xvi, 113–4
Council of Constance, ix
creeds, 28. *See also* Nicene Creed.
Cutsinger, James S., 27n8
Cyprian, St., 28, 48, 54, 97